Dedication

To my beautiful wife Brenda, our children, and life's sunshine - our terrific grandchildren.

Credits

Special thanks to Picture People portraits studio for their excellent photo shoots of Brenda on the front cover and other Talk to the Hand gestures. I would also like to acknowledge Clip Art for use of their illustrations that greatly enhanced the Talk to the Hand concepts. For more information, visit their respective websites at:

www.PicturePeople.com

www.ClipArt.com

Contents

Chapter

INTRODUCTION

"Everything should be made as simple as possible...but not simpler."[1]

Albert Einstein

If a concept is *simple*, we can remember it. If we can *remember* the concept, we can put into *practice*.

> The "talk to the hand" phrase is often associated with a dismissive attitude by the person holding up the hand. The opposite is true in this case. The stance portrayed on the book cover is in fact a positive one.

Early in my military career, as a First Lieutenant, I took charge of a 100-person Accounting and Finance Office. The diverse unit was comprised of enlisted personnel, young and seasoned civilians, and other officers. During that assignment, I admittedly made many mistakes in my first real test as an organizational leader.

My staff was supportive and forgiving while I rode a learning curve for three years. In many ways, what I learned from them became a benchmark from which to grow as a leader. They nominated me for what has turned out to be my most cherished individual award of my career – the Federal Woman's Program Male Boss of the Year.

I may not have had much experience but what I did know is at that moment, I vowed to start becoming a *learning leader* moving forward. This meant that I tried to analyze when things were going well (i.e., high morale in the unit), what was the root cause or causes? Similarly, if the organization seemed in a downward trend, why was that so? As John Wooden, the greatest coach of all time, once observed, "Longevity in leadership is related, in part, to your love of learning and the sense of urgency you attach to it."[2]

Over the next twenty plus years of leadership experience, I tried to synthesize my many observations of cause and effect into a few simple leadership tools that I could use in future and tougher assignments. These observations were from my direct experience as a leader, watching the successes and failures of leaders all around me, and through additional academic research while teaching a leadership course at the Air Force Academy.

The first leadership tool I developed into a book entitled, *The Leader's Pyramid: a balanced and consistent approach to leadership* (Authorhouse). In terms of simplicity, it is one of the few books that you can grasp the overall leadership concept by studying its front cover for a few moments.

~~~~~~~~~~~~

I believe that a leader can be a *great* leader by striving to be a person who exercises the numerous forms of power and influence at their disposal. A good balance among them is the key.

In this second book, *Talk to the Hand: being a great leader is at your fingertips*, I again offer a simple tool that can help any leader, new or experienced. The concept stems from and builds upon the five bases of power work done by John R.P. French Jr. and Bertram Raven in an article titled "The Bases of Social Power," in the *Studies of Social Power* (1959). While instructing at the Air Force Academy, I learned about the concept in the Leadership course textbook we used in our class. I acknowledge the visionary efforts and research of French and Raven on the subjects of power and influence.

The "talk to the hand" phrase is often associated with a dismissive attitude by the person holding up the hand. The opposite is true in this case. The stance portrayed on the book cover is in fact a positive one. My beautiful wife Brenda is demonstrating confidence and even eagerness that comes to a leader prepared to motivate others toward common success.

Instead of essentially telling *another* person to take a hike, "talk to the hand" in this case calls for *inward* reflection. I believe that a leader can be a *great* leader by striving to be a person who exercises the numerous forms of power at their disposal. A good balance among the influence factors is the key.

Being a leader is not easy, but it does not have to be hard.

Similarly, leadership concepts do not have to be complicated to be effective. I hope you enjoy and benefit from the Talk to the Hand leadership concept that works for me on a daily basis.

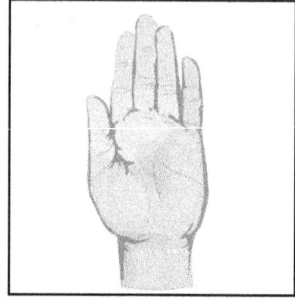

Chapter One

Gift of Fingers and Hands

"God's gifts put man's best dreams to shame."[3]

Elizabeth Barrett Browning

If you stop to think about it for a moment, a person can do some amazing things just by using God's gift of the fingers on our hands.

For example, imagine meeting your potential life mate based on only the use of your hands and fingers. Speed dating has become a means for people to interact quickly in a "round-robin" fashion in the hopes of finding a compatible match. At a recent speed-dating event, that took place at a Washington DC college, students gathered for the normal first-date conversation. Topics likely included such things as favorite hangouts, rating difficult professors, and determining common interests between the participants in normal "small talk."

Except on this Friday night, there was no actual talking in

the five-minute sessions – participants used only their fingers to communicate through sign language.[4]

What we can do using our Fingers and Hands

Before every football game, the referee uses a couple of fingers to toss a coin into the air to determine which team will have the choice of kicking off or receiving the ball.

When playing tennis, we use one set of fingers to throw a ball up in the air, and within a second we use another set to hit the ball on a serve with a tennis racket.

A baseball catcher can determine the best pitch to throw at the batter by merely flashing a few fingers downward to the pitcher 60 feet away.

Using his long fingers, President Abraham Lincoln dipped his pen in ink and moved his hand to sign the Emancipation Proclamation on New Year's Day, 1863. However, Lincoln's hand was trembling so he decided to put the pen down.[5]

The President was not second-guessing his own decision. He had in fact drafted the proclamation five months earlier and was waiting for the right time to sign it. The recent success at the Battle of Antietam granted him that opportunity.

The reason the President hesitated was that he had been shaking hands at the White House for three straight hours to greet New Year's Day visitors and his right arm was stiff. As he stated, "I never, in my life, felt more certain that I was doing right, than I do in signing this paper. If my name ever goes into history it will be for this act, and my whole soul is in it."[6]

Lincoln did not want someone who might examine the document *later* to declare that he had hesitated. After a moment, the President signed his name "slowly and carefully," and the result was a very clear, bold, and firm signature, even for Lincoln.[7]

Lincoln's legacy continued to make a difference nearly a century and a half later on another January day in Washington, DC. On January 20, 2009, Barack Obama raised his right hand and took the oath of office as the first African-American President in our nation's history.

In another example of the importance of our fingers and hands, Senator John McCain shares a poignant story about his days as a Prisoner of War captured in North Vietnam that involved a fellow prisoner (Mike) who was determined to sew an American flag.

Mike had humble origins growing up near Selma, Alabama and joined the Navy at seventeen. While captured, Mike used his fingers to make a needle out of bamboo, and gathered tiny scraps of red and white cloth. Careful to not to be caught by the watchful prison guards, he painstakingly sewed an American flag using the inside of his prisoner shirt (blue).[8]

As McCain recalls, "Every afternoon, before we ate our soup, we would hang Mike's flag on the wall of our cell and, together, recite the Pledge of Allegiance. No other event of the day had as much meaning to us."[9]

During a routine inspection, the prison guards discovered

Mike's flag and after confiscating it, came back later to beat him severely outside the cell. Mike's eardrum was punctured and several of his ribs were broken. After helping Mike crawl into bed, the prisoners settled in for the night. McCain recounts what he then saw underneath a dim bulb in a corner of the cell.[10]

"He (Mike) had crawled there quietly when he thought the rest of us were sleeping. With his eyes nearly swollen shut from the beating, he had quietly picked up his needle and thread and begun sewing a new flag."[11]

> ∿∿∿∿∿∿∿∿∿∿
>
> We do many things with our hands and fingers that we take for granted while we are doing them.

The *interaction* between another person's fingers and hands can lead to a bonding moment, such as occurs with a handshake or a salute.

Visiting Disneyland in Anaheim, California as a young boy, I ran to the sudden commotion nearby that had built up at the *It's a Small World* small boat tour attraction. As I arrived on scene, there was Robert F. Kennedy sitting on a boat exiting the ride with the rest of his family waving to the excited crowd. I joined in a line that had formed at the exit to get close contact with the popular Senator from New York. It was early June 1968.

RFK soon came by and stuck out his hand to me. As I shook his hand, I noticed how tired Bobby seemed. Looking back, that is understandable considering he was in the middle of a tough Democratic Party presidential nominee campaign and he was in California campaigning for that state's important delegate count. A few days later, shortly after giving a celebratory speech for winning the state's primary, Sirhan Sirhan, a disgruntled young Palestinian, gunned Bobby down for his support of Israel.

Many years later, I had the opportunity to participate in a send-off to President Bill Clinton at an Andrews Air Force Base hangar on the inauguration day of President George W. Bush. After his first speech as *former* President Clinton, he shook hands with those of us, mainly military members, in attendance. At the same event, I shook hands with Hillary and Chelsea Clinton as they also worked the line before boarding Air Force One for their final departure as the outgoing First Family.

We do many things with our hands and fingers that we take for granted while we are doing them. No thought goes into our gestures or hand movements because we are accustomed to using one or all of our fingers on our hands naturally.

Limitations When we *do not* use all Available Fingers

"After a while I thought it didn't make any sense to use a (guitar) pick. It's kind of like typing with one finger on each hand instead of using all your fingers."[12]

Kevin Eubanks

Jay Leno's musical sidekick (and guitarist)

When we have *unrestricted* access in using our fingers and hands, we do not even think about which finger to use, we do it naturally based on the need at the time. What happens when there are limits on our use of our fingers on our hands?

When I was a kid growing up, I had a BB rifle that I would shoot harmlessly in the back yard against targets such as tin cans. Sometimes after cocking the air rifle, I would not properly latch the lever handle and it would come crashing up against my fingers – causing me pain, swollen fingers, and such discomfort that I had to discontinue shooting.

I am sure most of you have faced a similar situation, where due to a minor accident or mishap, you could not freely use all of your fingers to do what you would normally take for granted.

In an example of how important *all* of our fingers are to us, Dallas Cowboys quarterback Tony Romo missed three full games after he broke his pinky finger and was unable to throw a pass. During his absence, the Cowboys team also felt the difference, losing two out of the three games.[13]

Washington Capitals hockey player Matt Bradley missed a month of playing hockey when he suffered a finger injury. "It's just a stupid little tip of your fingers keeping you out for a month, obviously very frustrating," he noted. During this time, the "Caps" also suffered a losing streak without Bradley.[14]

> ~~~~~~~~~~~
> There is *visible difference* between a
> leader who applies only one or two
> influence factors and a leader who uses
> their leadership capacity to the fullest.

The Signature Test

I asked my wife Brenda to write her signature using only two fingers – the middle finger and her ring finger. I watched as Brenda struggled to keep the pen stable and balanced. As a result, her writing below is choppy and does not represent her *true* signature.

Signature 1 (only middle and ring fingers):

I then asked Brenda to write her signature a second time but this time, using *all* her fingers. I noticed how she used some fingers directly to sign while others she used for support. Shown below is her second signature with her full set of fingers.

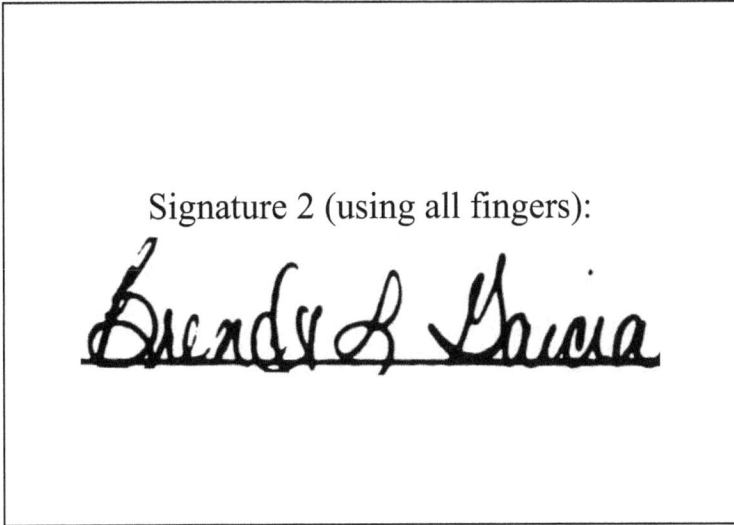

Signature 2 (using all fingers):

Brenda L. Garcia

Notice that Brenda's second signature, (the one with unlimited access of her fingers), is more naturally flowing than her first signature. Take a moment, and find a writing instrument and a blank piece of paper and try it yourself. Remember, for your first signature, you can only use the middle and ring fingers. Pull your other three fingers into a tight fist, with the other two sticking up like rabbit ears. No cheating.

Next, directly underneath your first signature, write your name as you would normally do so without thinking about it. Compare the two.

In most instances, there is a *visible difference between the two signatures*. The ensuing question becomes, why would you ever artificially *limit your ability* to perform (in this case, writing your signature)? Surprisingly, we do it all the time as leaders by not using our fullest capacity to influence others – the very heart of leadership. As leadership author and speaker John Maxwell once noted, "Leadership is influence."[15]

There is *visible difference* between a leader who applies only one or two influence factors and a leader who uses their leadership capacity to the fullest.

More importantly, there is also a *difference in their performance results as leaders.*

Chapter Two

Talk to the Hand Leadership Concept

"A basketball team is like the five fingers on your hand. If you can get them all together, you have a fist. That's how I want you to play."[16]

Mike Krzyzewski, Hall-of-Fame Duke Basketball Coach

In the same manner that we achieve more results by using all of our fingers instead of limiting ourselves to using less than all five, we limit our ability to influence others when we do not use all various powers of influence as a leader. The Talk to the Hand Leadership Concept uses our fingers to represent the five forms of influence and power that a leader possesses.

Thumb: As in "Thumbs up," – Rewards
Index finger: "Thinking" gesture – Sharing Knowledge
Middle finger: "Negative" gesture – Using Punishment
Ring finger: "Wedding ring" represents Status and Authority
Pinky: "Pinky shake" – Forging Relationships

17

The Talk to the Hand Leadership Concept is simple yet powerful. A leader who applies the whole spectrum of his or her influence (all five fingers in our analogy) will be more of an effective leader than the person who does not fully use what is at their disposal.

I have often seen leaders, however, who tend to emphasize primarily *two* factors; (1) *authority*, and (2) frequent use of *discipline*. The style is what I refer to as the "because I told you so" philosophy. Unfortunately, this leadership approach may be increasing rather than decreasing. In an article in *The Academy of Management Executive* entitled, "Putting people first for organizational success," Jeffrey Pfeffer and John Veiga noted the following:

"As global competition heats up and turmoil rocks more industries, tough management should spread. So look for more bosses who are steely, super demanding, unrelenting, sometimes abusive, sometimes unreasonable, impatient, driven, stubborn, and combative."[17]

Are these types of leaders more effective in the long run? My personal experience says no. Followers obey out of intimidation – not true loyalty. The strategy for the followers in this situation is to get through the day without a tongue-lashing or a negative encounter with the boss.

Notice that with our Talk to the Hand Leadership Concept,

the two factors of authority and discipline, are represented by the ring finger (legitimacy and authority based) and the middle finger (punishment and discipline) respectively. Referring back to the signature test, Brenda used only these two fingers for her first signature. The result is a less coherent signature when compared to her second attempt when she used all of her fingers on her hand.

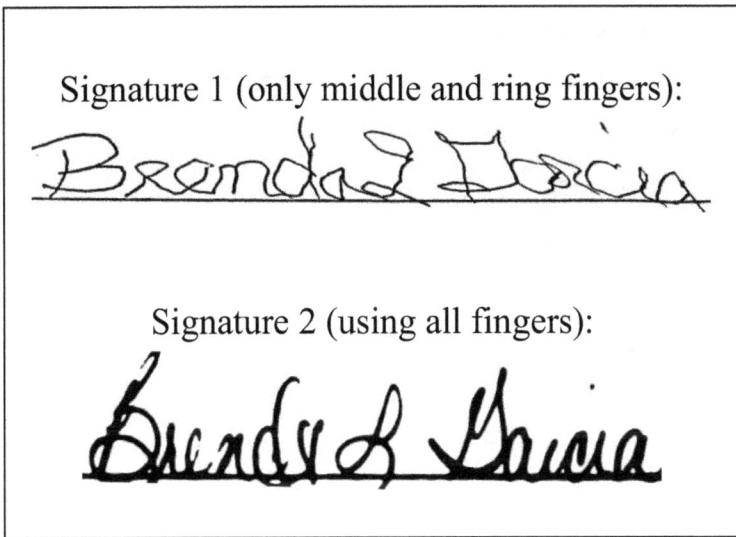

Signature 1 (only middle and ring fingers):

Signature 2 (using all fingers):

In the same manner, a manager who chooses only to lead by authority and punishment is not achieving maximum motivation and ability from their followers. Coach John Wooden once shared a story that illustrates this point.

Where Wooden grew up, there were gravel pits that the county would pay local farmers to haul out loads of gravel for use on the county roads. On one occasion, he observed a young farmer whipping and cursing a team of horses with a full load trying to ascend out of the gravel pit. The plow horses pulled back from the farmer, stomping and frothing at the mouth.[18]

Wooden's father, also at the scene, had seen enough and said to the young farmer, "Let me take 'em for you." When given the reins, he started talking to the horses and gently touching them. Without any use of a whip, or throwing a tantrum, he very calmly and gently led them out of the pit quite easily.[19]

Coach Wooden noted, "Over the years I've seen a lot of leaders act like that angry young farmer who lost control and resorted to force and intimidation. Their results were often the same, that is, no results."[20]

"If a leader's horse fails to obey him, it is because his fingers fail to obey him."[21]

Bil Holton, *Leadership Lessons of Robert E. Lee*

In our "because I told you so" management example, followers are less likely to be motivated because there is *nothing* motivating them. For motivation, what is missing is some type of rewards (giving a thumbs up), or establishing a personal relationship with the follower (pinky connection). If you are not sharing your knowledge (demonstrated by the index finger to the brain), there is less means to enhance follower ability.

A leadership formula that I developed that has worked for me over the years is the MAP formula; Motivation times Ability equals Performance (shown below).

MAP Formula

Motivation (M) X Ability (A) = Performance (P)

By concentrating only on the *right side* of the equation (Performance), a leader is merely looking at an outcome or a result. The MAP formula suggests that a leader should instead concentrate on the *left side* of the equation, Motivation and Ability. A leader can influence both of the two factors that really *determine* performance[22]

Therefore, a leader should seek 100 percent Motivation *and* Ability from their followers to attain maximum Performance. When you have a follower that is completely (100 percent) Motivated and 100 percent Able, you not leaving any Performance capability behind.

Using our MAP formula to quantify the "because I told you so" management approach, motivation is probably low (say 60 percent) and follower ability is relatively low (70 percent). Performance in this case is in the 40 percent range (70 percent X 60 percent is 42 percent).

On the other hand, a leader who uses the full range of influence at their disposal is a powerful force indeed. Using all your fingers (symbolizing power factors of rewards, knowledge sharing, punishment, authority, and rewards) is most likely to attain the highest levels of both follower Motivation *and* Ability.

Let me be clear, I am *not* suggesting that we completely ignore the use of our legitimate authority (ring finger) or the ability to discipline (middle finger). They are part of the overall leadership hand, and leaders need to use all of their forms of influence appropriately.

In the following examples, we use various fingers or a combination of them to make gestures or take other actions.

To throw a Frisbee – thumb, middle, and index fingers

Make music (piano, flute, etc) – every finger is used

"Call me" gesture – thumb and pinky

Vulcan salute – All used but middle and ring fingers parted

Text a message – normally thumbs

Operating a TV remote – thumb and other fingers

Shake hands – all fingers

Putting a thread into a needle – thumb and Index fingers

Putting in your eye contacts – index and middle fingers

These few examples demonstrate a logical and natural balance among all or a combination of fingers used. Using one finger or several does not limit your ability to use the others later.

In the same manner, a leader should strive to use the full range of his or her power and influence according to the situation at hand. In doing so, followers are likely to have high Motivation and high Ability. As a result, Performance will also be high.

Now that we have described the Talk to the Hand Leadership Concept generally, we can be more specific for each of the individual elements of power and influence demonstrated by our fingers.

Let's get started Talking to the Hand.

Chapter Three

Thumbs Up: Using Rewards

"Leaders who figure out, on their own, ways to reward their people for good performance get more good performance than leaders who run around all day putting out fires caused by their people's poor performance."[23]

Steve Chandler, from the book *100 Ways to Motivate Others*

~~~~~~~~~~~

Not using rewards would be like not using your thumb – reducing your ability to use your hand to the fullest capacity.

During World War II, American pilots would give their *thumb up* signal to communicate to their ground crews that everything was in order and they were ready to take off. The pilots likely borrowed the gesture from an old Chinese custom used to express respect, as in "you're number one." In our Talk to the Hand concept, the thumb up represents use of rewards for a job well done.

> ~~~~~~~~~~
> See how far you can throw a football without being able to use your thumb on your hand.

There are those who believe that rewards in themselves are in fact a negative influence on people instead of a positive one. The logic goes like this, "Distributing rewards serves to control others – not influence them." Using rewards is considered de-humanizing, treating people like pets."[24]

I disagree that rewards are controlling or de-humanizing. As part of a person's ability to influence others toward continued success, the capacity to reward is vital to a leader. Not using rewards would be like not using your thumb – reducing your ability to use your hand to the fullest capacity.

See how far you can throw a football without being able to use your thumb on your hand. Without the use of his thumb, Boston College quarterback Doug Flutie would not have been able to throw his famous "Hail Mary" pass nearly 70 yards as the game clock wound down to beat the University of Miami Hurricanes on November 23, 1984.

Similarly, without the use of rewards, a leader is less capable of achieving maximum results. As John Kotter, respected management author and former Harvard Business School professor once noted, "… good leaders recognize and reward success, which not only gives people a sense of accomplishment but also makes them feel like they belong to an organization that cares about them."[25]

Hurricane Katrina Experience using Rewards

> ~~~~~~~~~~
> I thought it was only fair that the thousands of FEMA term employees assigned to various Recovery Offices, working very long hours, and making a difference to their fellow Americans, should receive a performance bonus.

As the FEMA "Katrina CFO" in New Orleans, Louisiana for three years, I witnessed some exceptional work from the dedicated employees across the Gulf Coast to support long-term recovery. Despite the negative stigma that is associated with FEMA's efforts, I saw many successful local stories that never made the national headlines.

When I would wear my FEMA shirt, many people in the Gulf Coast would come up to merely thank me as a FEMA representative. They appreciated the temporary living quarters and financial assistance that went to them, their families, and to rebuilding their schools and communities.

A significant number of employees in the workforce were themselves survivors of Hurricane Katrina. Like their neighbors, many of them lost everything to the terrible 2005 "storm of the century." Hiring these people on the FEMA payroll was one means to assist in the local recovery since many of them lost their jobs due to the storm. More importantly, who better to show empathy to an individual or community requiring assistance than people who have been there and walked in their shoes?

I thought it was only fair that the thousands of FEMA employees assigned to various Recovery Offices, working very long hours, and making a difference to their fellow Americans, should receive a performance bonus. The problem was that like many issues related to Hurricane Katrina; we were on new ground for many of them. Some in FEMA headquarters were concerned of the potential perception of using disaster funds for performance bonuses.

Teaming with the Gulf Coast Administrator in New Orleans, I successfully lobbied for and won approval for funds to pay small bonuses to the top performers in recognition of their outstanding support. It was the right thing to do.

Overseas Experience using Rewards

As leaders, we need to be creative in providing the recognition and rewards that can be a motivator to exceed expectations as the following stories demonstrate.

"I was tired, but I couldn't give up."

The week I arrived at Ramstein Air Base, Germany to take charge of the largest Finance Office in Europe was by coincidence the week that the unit was conducting the annual aerobics fitness test. At that time, the test was a one and a half mile run against a certain standard based on your age and gender.

As soon as I heard about the fitness test, I issued a challenge to my new unit. *Anyone who could beat the new Captain would receive a one-day pass.* Despite being older than the majority of the younger troops, I was an avid runner, who had lettered in track (long distance) and cross-country in high school. I figured that at most only a few could outdo me and that it would be a good morale booster for the unit.

The morning of the run, I surveyed the large group of runners for who might have a chance of beating me and winning the day off. There was a handful or so that looked in running shape that could beat me. I normally ran the one and a half-mile run in about nine and a half minutes.

As the run commenced, I settled in to a normal stride to find a good rhythm of pace and breathing. Some of the troops that were ahead of me early in the run, I figured would inevitably slow down and that I would easily pass them as we wound through the course.

At the midway point, only three runners were ahead of me out of nearly one hundred that had started the run. The first two looked like they were in good shape and I would unlikely be able to catch up to them. However, I had my sights on the one Airman immediately in front of me, known as "Skip".

"Skip" was about 6'2" and 225 pounds, and looked more like a football lineman than a runner compared to the others leading the pack. I thought for sure that he would begin to slow down and fall back as the race wore on. With only a few hundred yards to go, I began to make my move and mustered a kick towards the finish line in sight. As I increased my pace, "Skip" kept looking over his shoulder and sped up so I never could catch him. To my surprise, Skip beat me soundly and ran a very fast time for a man his size.

After the race, I walked over to shake the hands of those who had beaten me. When I congratulated "Skip," I confessed to him that I thought for sure he was going to "die" and fade. The young troop looked at me and said, "I kept thinking about that one day off pass you had offered if we could beat you. I was tired, but I couldn't give up. I really wanted that one day pass."

Perhaps not everyone felt as "Skip" had about running hard just for one day off. He gained more than just time off though, "Skip" gained bragging rights over me that he could playfully throw my way when the occasion warranted. To me, that was fine too, as it would motivate *me* to do better next time.

> ~~~~~~~~~~~
> Rewards do not always have to be costly
> or time consuming to administer to make
> a difference to your staff.

During the same overseas assignment, a young man named Jeff won a very significant award, Airman of the Year for the 316th Air Division at Ramstein Air Base, Germany. The award signified that he was the "best of the best" out of several hundred Airmen in his grade category.

The Superintendent (a Chief Master Sergeant), and I submitted a good package on Jeff for him to win at numerous levels (Squadron, Group, Wing, etc) before winning at the Division level. In reality, we had the easy part by putting all his achievements on paper. Jeff was the one who looked like a poster boy in uniform. He also had done a great job in Military Pay customer service as evidenced by many positive comments we received by customers.

One day, during small talk, we discovered that Jeff thought it would be great to take a flight in the F-16 fighter jet. The "Fighting Falcon" is the plane that the United States Air Force Thunderbirds fly in as they tour throughout the world as Air Force ambassadors.

The fighter jet can go vertical after take- off in a matter of a few seconds and reach supersonic speed. At that time, the mission at Ramstein included a fighting capability, and several F-16 squadrons were located on base. Jeff, like the rest of us, routinely saw the planes screaming overhead.

The Chief Master Sergeant began working his magic and before long, Jeff was viewing the beautiful Germany countryside in the backseat of an F-16 fighter jet. To this day, I am not sure who was more excited about the incentive flight—me, the Chief, or Jeff himself.

The F-16 fighter jet incentive flight for Jeff admittedly was extraordinary and special to obtain, probably a once in a lifetime event. As we will see, however, rewards do not always have to be costly or time consuming to administer to make a difference to your staff.

Offer "Cake" and a "Break"

Now that we have determined that use of rewards is an important source of influence a leader can use to motivate, we can concentrate on what types of rewards to use. There are two types of rewards: "cake" is something tangible *consumed* in the short term. Examples of "cake" rewards are time off, money, and a simple "thank you". On the other hand, offering a "break" is an opportunity for longer-term success such as challenging work or a career move. Both types are important to *dish out*, and both are very meaningful to those receiving them.

During tough economic times, managers may try to cut back on reward programs citing that they can no longer afford them. In other cases, management does not even bother with rewards and recognition for the organization, citing other higher priorities. Even if you cannot afford to give a whole cake, at least offer up a *slice of cake*, whether it is one *hour*, one *hundred dollars*, or one *thank* you – small rewards can go a long way.

> A tangible reward is important because the followers offered something tangible to earn the incentive in the first place.

A Slice of Cake – Time-Off Reward

In our fast-paced world, we seldom have time to just relax or do things that refresh our spirit. Even on weekends, we often go from one end of town to the other running errands such as picking up laundry, going to the bank, cleaning the house or working on the yard, and other "chores" that are part of everyday life.

When I was a squadron commander, if the unit was performing well and meeting our mission objectives, I tried to reward them. I would occasionally send out an email message thanking the team for their hard work and efforts and grant them an hour off to end their day early. You may wonder what could an hour mean in a person's day and why bother doing so? The answer might surprise you.

Here are 20 activities people could engage in with *one hour* off:

1. Get a manicure

2. Beat traffic home

3. Go grocery shopping

4. Visit the library and browse the books and magazines

5. Workout at the gym (beat the after-work crowd)

6. Take a walk in the park

7. Get your car washed

8. Mow the lawn

9. Go to the mall

10. Visit a sick friend

11. Pick up the kids from school rather than taking the bus

12. Catch up on homework for a college night-time course

13. Take a power nap

14. Run small errands normally done on a weekend

15. Grab a cup of coffee and read the newspaper

16. Make a special dinner for the family

17. Go to the driving range and hit a bucket of golf balls

18. Take a walk on the beach

19. Watch an afternoon TV show

20. Do nothing

As you can see, granting one-hour time off or early release could be a highly motivational tool. Suppose you chose to grant an hour off six times a year. If the average employee works 40 hours a week X 50 weeks (allowing for two weeks vacation), that would be approximately 2,000 hours in a work year.

Granting six one-hour time offs as rewards per year would amount to $6/2000^{th}$ or 0.003 time away from the job, only *about $1/3^{rd}$ of one percent* for the average work year. Raising morale and motivation for such a small reward is a great return on investment. In the manner that a small amount of time-off can make a big difference, the same holds true for monetary rewards.

A Slice of Cake – Money

~~~~~~~~~~~~

Many followers told me *my own thought and effort* to yield the reward was more important to them than the actual incentives.

Not long ago, I worked as a Team Lead for a contractor supporting a federal government client in Washington, DC. One of our big deliverables was an assessment over their internal controls. Instead of just leaving the client with a list of write-ups, we wanted to go a step further by producing tangible recommendations and solutions to fix some of the problem areas we had documented.

To that end, our team worked very hard for several months and was very creative in our proposed implementation plan. The government client favorably received the final report, and implemented most of our team's recommendations.

Although we were essentially fulfilling a contractual requirement, I thought the team had gone above-and-beyond with their efforts.

I coordinated with my boss and won approval to issue a one-hundred dollar bonus in the next paycheck for each team member. The small amount may not seem like much (just as an hour off might to some), but I wanted the team to know how much I appreciated their effort and wanted to demonstrate it tangibly with the small bonus.

As in the case with the power of one hour off, let us see

what the power of one hundred dollars might do. Here are 20 *items* you could purchase with *one hundred dollars*:

1. Flowers sent to a loved one for no reason
2. Tickets for a sporting event
3. Pocket Camcorder
4. Several entertainment videos
5. Dinner and a movie for two
6. A round of golf and lunch (at most courses)
7. Car professionally detailed
8. Junior golf club set
9. An infant car seat
10. A full body one-hour massage
11. Oil change and tire rotation
12. New pair of running shoes
13. New color printer for the home office
14. Stainless steel blender for the kitchen
15. Three or four new books
16. $100 dollar gift certificate
17. A new outfit
18. A new lamp
19. Knife-set with wood block
20. New sports-watch

A small but unexpected amount of time off or monetary reward can go a long way towards motivating your followers. Recently, I formed five working groups, comprised of office volunteers, to make recommendations on our new organizational strategic plan. Each team consisted of approximately seven persons and addressed the following areas:

- Recognition
- Training
- Professional Development
- Morale
- Communication

The groups spent a lot of time and effort that included building and delivering a final presentation to the senior staff and me. In the end, we incorporated nearly all of their recommendations into our final strategic plan. As a small token of appreciation, I arranged for all of the group members to receive a $100 dollar bonus *and* an 8-hour time off award.

I received several e-mails from the award recipients expressing their own appreciation, including the following:

Joe

We wanted to thank you for the unexpected award of time off and money. It was very much appreciated and very unexpected.

Thanks again,

The Morale Group

A Slice of Cake — Thanks

"There are two things people want more than sex and money — recognition and praise."[26]

Mary Kay Ash, Founder, Mary Kay Cosmetics, Inc.

A tangible reward is important because the followers offered something tangible to earn the incentive in the first place. In my last example, the five strategic plan working groups produced recommendations that were eventually incorporated, including developing a mentorship program, and establishing a "brown bag" professional development series.

As important as giving rewards such as time off and/or money, is the intangible *payment* of appreciation and thanks. People need to understand, when the occasion warrants it, that you acknowledge their good performance. A leader can effectively demonstrate thanks through a variety of means.

Through Email

Email is effective when you want to recognize group success such as exceeding targets. An email is also appropriate when your group is scattered across geographical locations that make meeting in one place a challenge. Quick emails to recognize an individual's effort is okay but balance your approach using other methods.

Thank You or Praise Cards or Notes

"If each of us were to confess his most secret desire, the one that inspires all his plans, all his actions, he would say: 'I want to be praised.'"[27]

E.M. Cioran

I once worked for a commander who used to send thank you notes on personalized cards when an individual went above-and-beyond on the job. For example, customers would occasionally recognize someone from our unit for providing exceptional customer service. The commander would often send a thank you card as a result to express her appreciation. The personal card was a nice touch because the person receiving the card could pass it along for others to see.

Phone call

Although an email or a thank you card is a good gesture, calling someone on the phone to express thanks and appreciation is a special touch. Actually *hearing* the words forms a personal connection between you and the individual(s) who warranted the effort. We sometimes hear in the news, when the President of the United States will use this technique, by calling someone to express gratitude or praise for a special accomplishment.

Personal Visit

Making a phone call to offer your personal thanks or praise is a special gesture, but whenever possible a personal visit is even better. Personally visiting someone in the work area shows that you are in tune with what is happening at the "shop level." The personal visit also offers a firm handshake and perhaps a photo opportunity.

"As a society we have come to rely far too much on impersonal modes of communication. Email and texting are fine for transmitting data such as 'Meet u at Strbcks at 11.' But if you want to solve problems or inspire the troops, you've got to communicate face-to-face. Your followers need more than just your words glowing on a computer screen. They need to see the passion in your eyes and the intensity in your gestures and body language."[28]

Pat Williams, Vice-President and Co-Founder, Orlando Magic

Presentations at Staff Meeting

My personal favorite to thank someone or offer praise for a job well done is at a staff meeting. Before moving on to the official agenda, I would always recognize deserving individuals first. For example, if a customer took the time to write a nice letter of appreciation, I would endorse the letter and personally hand it out at the weekly staff meeting.

The staff meeting is normally the place where the senior team gathers, so why not use the forum to recognize individuals and put a *spotlight* on their achievement. This type of forum allows for a photo op (you and the recipient shaking hands) that you could display on a unit photo board for other team members to see.

Providing an Opportunity (a Break)

Although offering up *cake* as a form of reward is important, equally important is offering a "break" or an opportunity, for your employees. In that regard, I owe much to my good friend and mentor L.C. Williams for providing me numerous *breaks* throughout my career.

I first met L.C. when assigned to Osan Air Base, Republic of Korea (South Korea). L. C. served as the Accounting and Finance Officer and I was his Deputy. For nearly a year, we worked hard together in a tough remote assignment. Since then, we remained the best of friends.

A few years after our South Korean assignment, L.C. was in

Europe assigned to the headquarters at Ramstein Air Base, Germany. I was finishing a tour in Texas and looking for a challenging next tour. L.C. wrote and sent me a list of bases that would have available assignments for Accounting and Finance Officers the next summer.

When I received L.C's letter, I saw that Ramstein was on the list. It was by far the largest Air Force installation in Europe and I wrote L.C. back that I wanted to pursue Ramstein for my next assignment because it looked like a challenge. It was home to a fighter wing, and the European headquarters resided on the base. L.C., a Major at the time, wrote back a second time that *all* overseas assignments were challenging and do not worry about the size of the operation.

Possessing a healthy ego, I wrote back; "If you are going to be in the circus, you might as well play under the big top." L.C. had his work cut out from his end because the current Finance Officer at Ramstein was a Major and I was a junior Captain. The Ramstein account, considered one of the toughest ones in the Air Force due to its size and historical complexity, needed an experienced officer at the helm.

Yet, my friend L.C. supported me despite my large ego and pushed hard to give me a *break* that turned out well in the long term. That one assignment set me up for future success in my career. During that same assignment, I returned the favor and provided career opportunities for two young enlisted persons.

"Getting Promoted Should Mean Something"

Enlisted personnel promotions in the Air Force are through several factors, including; performance reports, formal awards (medals), time in current grade, length of service, and testing. In my experience, one of the tougher promotions is the step from Staff Sergeant to Technical or Tech Sergeant.

Gayle, a relatively young Staff Sergeant, earned her promotion to Tech Sergeant ahead of the normal timeline. She was sharp, knowledgeable, and an excellent Non-Commissioned Officer (NCO). After receiving a promotion line number, Gayle needed to wait her turn (about six months) until the people with a higher line number pinned on their new stripes.

I spoke with our Superintendent, a Chief Master Sergeant, and together we planned what new responsibilities Gayle could assume when she pinned on the Technical Sergeant Stripes. My thoughts were that "getting promoted should mean something." I wanted others in the unit to see that when Gayle reached her personal milestone, there should be a change. To continue doing the same job she had as a Staff Sergeant would be inappropriate in my mind.

One of the most important areas to me is customer service. At Ramstein Air Base, our customer area unit serviced approximately 10,000 military assigned to the largest Air Force installation in Europe. How people gauged our entire 150-person Accounting and Finance Office, in both performance and reputation, often went the way of our customer service function.

In order to create efficiency and more effectiveness, we merged our Military Pay unit with our Travel Pay section into one combined customer service counter area. It was a bit risky because there was a lot of moving parts associated with both functions but I had done so successfully in my previous stateside assignment.

After consulting with the Chief, we decided that the day Gayle pinned on Technical Sergeant, would be the day she officially took responsibility as NCO-in-Charge (NCOIC) of the Customer Service Unit. At a relatively junior rank, she would be responsible for supporting the largest number of customers in the Air Force for someone in her military grade.

When the Chief and I called Gayle in to announce the move, she was a bit surprised, and somewhat apprehensive. She knew firsthand the importance of the customer service function to both our office and to the entire base. If things bogged down, everybody from pilots who needed to be in the air, to headquarters staff with oversight of the entire European theater, would feel the impact.

In the weeks and days leading up to the big day, we supported Gayle with words of encouragement and positive reinforcement. We felt that this *break* (opportunity) could mean a lot to her career down the road. The potential write-up for her performance reports and award citations if she performed well were significant.

It came as no surprise that Gayle did perform as expected. She took advantage of her big *break* and went on to become a Chief Master Sergeant in her own right years later. Congress authorizes only one percent of the enlisted force to obtain this highest rank. I am confident that Gayle looked for similar opportunities for enlisted personnel *she* supervised throughout the remainder of her career.

The Youngest Deputy

~~~~~~~~~~
I was demonstrating to the entire enlisted corps that when they had made the necessary sacrifices to earn their stripes, then whenever possible, there came additional responsibilities and challenges to along with their increased rank.

During the same Germany assignment, another female Staff Sergeant named Shawn worked hard to earn her *"break"*. Unlike Gayle who worked in a highly visible customer service area, Shawn was assigned to our Disbursing function, working literally behind a secure door.

The Disbursing area's primary responsibility was to pay all of the commercial vendors and suppliers that provided services and materials to Ramstein Air Base. The Deputy also ensured thousands of individuals received their payroll and travel payments in cash or checks in a timely manner.

As the Accounting and Finance Officer, I was authorized to assign several Deputies in the Disbursing area. In this capacity, the Deputies could certify payments on my behalf. It was an important responsibility, normally served by a more senior NCO or even an officer.

Shawn had proven herself to me because of her loyalty, commitment, and great work ethic. The day that we found out that she had earned her line number for Technical Sergeant, I had something special in mind for her big *break*. I planned to make Shawn the most junior (in rank) Deputy in the history of the largest Accounting and Finance Office in Europe.

Unlike my decision for Gayle to assume leadership of our combined customer service unit, this one would require European headquarters approval. The regulations clearly stated that a Deputy Accounting and Finance Officer (DAFO) serving in the Disbursing section should be a higher rank because of all the cash related responsibilities. A special waiver from the headquarters was required for a Technical Sergeant to serve in that capacity.

My initial lobbying to assign Shawn as a Deputy met some resistance. The Ramstein operation was a complex account and placing such a junior ranking person as a DAFO was highly unusual. I stuck to my guns and prepared the formal waiver request. As soon as Shawn pinned on her new stripes, I walked over the package personally to begin the review process.

It would take continual pressure on the headquarters to approve Shawn's designation as a Deputy AFO. Soon, however, Technical Sergeant "Shawn" became Deputy AFO "Shawn." Again, I wanted a promotion to mean something.

I was demonstrating to the entire enlisted corps that when they had made the necessary sacrifices to earn their stripes, then whenever possible, there came additional responsibilities and challenges that went along with their increased rank. Shawn had earned her break just as Gayle had earned hers. As in the case with Gayle's success as the customer service chief, Shawn would serve with distinction in her new duties. It was a win-win situation for her and the entire office.

PEP Rally in the States

When I became a Squadron Commander, in addition to meeting each person for a quick introduction, I scheduled a 30-minute meeting for each individual assigned to the unit. It took me a while but I finally was able to meet with all 70 squadron members. There was positive buzz that the new boss took the time to meet with the highest- ranking person as well as the lowest-ranking one. In addition to getting to know more about them, such as their goals, family, hobbies, etc, the exchanges allowed me to get a sense of what the organizational strengths were along with areas for improvement.

Although there were no major problems to speak of, the squadron members felt there could be opportunity for promotion and advancement. I dug deeper and found there was a legitimate cause for concern. For example, from my experience, the civilian grade levels were relatively low. Additionally, there was no "corporate ladder" to climb from the lowest grade to the highest. There were plenty of level-5 graded positions, but a gap existed at the middle grades (particularly 6 and 7 positions) to gain experience and be competitive for the higher grades. As a result, many workers sought employment elsewhere on the installation where there were better promotion opportunities.

~~~~~~~~~~~

Quick emails to recognize an individual's effort is okay but balance your approach using other methods.

In order to improve on this situation, I created an initiative called the Professional Enhancement Program, or PEP. I recruited volunteers to serve on a committee that would develop the necessary elements for the new program. PEP consisted of four elements, or pillars, that would work in unison to provide *breaks* for the workforce to achieve their professional ambitions. The four pillars consisted of organizational alignment, education, training, and PEP talks (figure 1).

Professional Enhancement Program (PEP) pillars			
Organizational Alignment	Off-Duty Education	Training Program	PEP Talks

Figure 1

Organizational Alignment

Over an organization's lifetime, we tend to put *band-aids* on problems instead of addressing the root causes. Too often, we *manage by personality* instead of doing is what is right for the mission. I worked hand-in-hand with the base Human Resources Office to review our organizational structure.

We reevaluated position descriptions and grade levels to factor in the advances made in technology and business processes. The result of this fresh perspective and analysis was the ability to create grade levels that provided better opportunities.

Concurrently to properly aligning the organization, we needed to ensure the workforce had the right tools to be eligible for advancement.

Off-Duty Education

Completing a formal education had changed my life years ago. Through encouragement of my peers, as a young enlisted man, I started taking evening college courses. Eventually, I received my degree and a commission as an officer in the Air Force. This time, however, my workforce needed that same type of opportunity I received early in my own career.

During this time, I was teaching online courses on a part-time basis. I invited representatives from the university to meet with our squadron members. To sweeten the deal, I encouraged the university to offer a 25 percent tuition discount to those who enrolled in their pilot program. As a result, over 20 individuals signed up for the online program and made a significant headway towards completing their educational pursuits.

Training Program

Building an effective training program takes some work but creates the win-win situation a leader desires. I assigned a Training NCO to help add a focus and structure to our training program.

In addition to the normal job-related training, I encouraged classes on everything from customer service to leadership and management. We established a monthly training plan and I received a regular report on our progress.

PEP Talks

The fourth pillar of the Professional Enhancement Program was what I used to call *PEP talks*. I invited senior leaders from around our installation to speak directly to our organization. On those occasions, the whole squadron gathered to hear a "pep talk" from someone who had reached the top of his or her profession.

For example, one General Officer shared the importance of honesty and integrity. During another occasion, a Colonel encouraged the team to establish and strive for their goals as he had done. During another pep talk, a Chief Master Sergeant shared tips on how he had achieved the highest enlisted rank by never being satisfied with his performance.

Not all the PEP talks were motivational in nature. Some had a practical application. For example, I invited the Auditor in charge of the regional office to share with the group what it would take to become an auditor and he even unveiled an intern program for those who were interested.

All of the elements built on each other, and in my mind, were equally important. The results of the PEP program were impressive. Several of our employees became Auditors. A young enlisted person now has her commission as an officer. Finally, nearly 40 percent of the squadron's civilians received promotions, permanent status, or a large severance pay.

> Just as a thumb is not the only finger on your hand, using rewards is *not the only way to influence.*

Final thoughts on use of Rewards

Offering tangible rewards such as *cake* (time-off, money, and simple thanks) is important because your followers offered something tangible to earn the incentive. If your resources are limited, even a *slice* of cake, such as an hour time-off or a hundred dollars makes a difference. Of course, saying a simple "thank you" is free yet the impact is also great. In addition to offering cake, make sure to offer your people a *break*. This will take more of an effort on your part as demonstrated by the PEP program example.

If you already have a vibrant rewards program, keep it up. If you have one that could use a makeover, by all means, look at ways to make it better.

Just as a thumb is not the only finger on your hand, using rewards is *not the only way to influence*.

Maintain a good balance among all the influence factors to be successful. In the next chapter, we will analyze how acquiring and sharing our knowledge with others is another important attribute for a leader.

Chapter Four

Index Finger: Sharing Knowledge

"In today's environment, hoarding knowledge ultimately erodes your power, if you know something very important, the way to get power is by actually sharing it."[29]

Joseph Badaracco, Harvard Business School Professor

Francis Bacon once said, "Knowledge is power." When someone points with his or her index finger to their head, the gesture usually means that the person is thinking hard about an issue, or has come up with a good idea – an "aha" moment. In our case, we use the index finger to represent that a leader possesses sufficient corporate and job knowledge, or general comprehension, that can be valuable to the organization or to others in it. A leader has three objectives when it comes to using knowledge as an element of power and influence:

- Acquire knowledge
- Share the knowledge
- Build trust so that the knowledge is readily received

Leader's Goal in Knowledge Sharing		
Acquire knowledge	*Share knowledge*	*Be trusted so knowledge is received*

"Left unattended, knowledge and skill, like all assets, depreciate in value – surprisingly quickly."[30]

David Maister

The Need to stay Ahead of the Group

One of my favorite military assignments involved teaching a Leadership course as an adjunct instructor at the Air Force Academy in Colorado Springs, Colorado. This was no easy task. Sitting in the classroom were some of our nation's most capable and brightest individuals. I remember what a friend and fellow instructor once told me at a department faculty meeting, "You need to always stay ahead of the students."

He explained that an effective instructor could not just follow the syllabus and go over the assigned readings every class. If that was the case, what *additional value* did you bring into the classroom? The students could do the same themselves. My friend encouraged me to do additional research so that I could do more than just repeat what was in the instructor's guide.

Through continuous preparation and effort on my part, I *acquired sufficient knowledge* to stay ahead of my group of students. I got into a habit of reading leadership books and articles, in addition to our formal textbook. The morning I taught class, I woke up at 4 a.m. to read the morning newspaper and see if I could use any of the current events to emphasize a topic for that day's lesson. I also worked on effectively communicating, or *sharing the knowledge*, to the students.

Whenever possible, I showed movie video clips to drive home a key leadership topic. I even invited guest speakers to the class to share their experiences and expertise on various lessons.

Finally, I *earned the trust* of my class through a variety of means. Whether attending their athletic events, becoming a mentor to them, or treating them with respect and courtesy, they knew that I had their best interests in mind. Without trust, no matter how much knowledge I had acquired to share with my students, they would not be sufficiently open to receive it.

In our Talk to the Hand analogy, not using and sharing knowledge would be like not being able to use you index finger. The following gestures or actions would be limited or impossible without the use of your index finger.

- Making a "We're number one" gesture

- Typing on the keyboard

- Flashing a "peace" or "victory" sign

The same principles hold true for a leader in the workplace. A leader who does not possess *sufficient knowledge to stay ahead of the group* has less impact and influence on others.

Acquiring Knowledge

"There is a deep, yet subtle, truth in the Latin expression, "Nemo dat quod non habet," which translates as "You cannot give what you do not have". The question, therefore, is how does a leader obtain that which he is obliged to pass along?"[31]

Chaplain (Col) Ray Fairman

A leader acquires knowledge through various forms, and in doing so, is able to be ahead of the group. A leader can obtain knowledge through education, certifications, personal experience or experience of others, and from exposure to information received by the nature of the leader's position or perch.

Acquiring Knowledge through Formal Education

"For years, people have recognized the value of a four-year degree, but to succeed in today's economy, you really need a forty-year degree. In other words, you need to be engaged in lifelong learning."[32]

Stephen M.R. Covey, from the book, *The Speed of Trust*

While assigned at the Air Force Academy, I witnessed a direct correlation between the knowledge gained and the leader's advancement. Within a 24-hour period, the cadets attended a commencement ceremony to receive their Bachelors of Science degree diploma and in another ceremony, they received their commissions as Second Lieutenants. In this case, *knowledge*, in the form of a formal education, *led to immediate advancement*.

For the rest of us, although not as instantaneous, completing a four-year degree still opens doors. In order for a leader to *be ahead of the group*, he or she must look at learning as a continuous venture. As Robert E. Lee once noted, "The education of a man is never completed until he dies."[33] Pursuing the next level of education is important to stay abreast of technology and business practices in your chosen career field and general management techniques. Admittedly, it is not always an easy thing to do with the demands of career and family.

When accepted to serve as the "Hurricane Katrina CFO" in New Orleans for the FEMA, my wife Brenda and I moved from the Washington, D.C. area to the Gulf Coast in August 2006. At the time, I was about halfway through an Executive Masters in Leadership program at Georgetown University. I thought it only fair to the Gulf Coast Recovery Administrator to focus entirely on our important recovery mission immediately upon arrival.

After one year, however, I arranged with Georgetown to pick up the Masters program at the point I had left off earlier.

Fortunately, the curriculum was the same so the classes I did not finish from the previous year were still the ones offered for this year's students.

Getting permission to continue the program from Georgetown and FEMA superiors turned out to be the easy part, the hard part was in trying to finish it. The Georgetown University Executive Masters in Leadership is the only Master's degree program of its kind offered by a prominent business school and university. Classes were held every other weekend – on Fridays from 1:00 pm-8:30 pm and on Saturdays from 8:30 am-4:30 pm.

For over four months, every other Friday afternoon, I would wake up at 2a.m. to drive from Biloxi, Mississippi to the New Orleans airport and catch the earliest possible flight across country to be in class on time. Unlike most of the other students who resided in the DC area, I then had to worry about finding a place to stay during the weekend.

The extra expense of round-trip airfare, rental cars, lodging, and food twice per month was an additional financial burden to manage. In the end, it was all worth the effort. Oftentimes, I would return to work on Monday and put in practice an idea or concept learned from the previous weekend. Pursuing the Georgetown Masters program met my objective of *acquiring knowledge to stay ahead of the group*. Although formal education is an important means to do so, it is by no means the only way.

> ~~~~~~~~~~~~
> By obtaining a professional certification,
> you become an expert in your field.

Acquiring Knowledge through Professional Certifications

Continuing your formal education is important because you acquire a *breadth of knowledge* across the full spectrum: natural sciences, social sciences, mathematics, English, behavioral sciences, and the arts. Pursuing a professional certification is also important as a means to acquire the appropriate *depth of knowledge* in your particular career field. In addition to completing my Masters from Georgetown University while serving as the Katrina CFO in New Orleans, I also obtained certification as a Certified Government Financial Manager (CGFM). Sponsored by the Association of Government Accountants (AGA), the certification represents the wide range of knowledge and skills that a professional financial manager needs to succeed at all levels of government.

Many certifications require a minimum number of years in professional-level experience, completion of at least a Bachelor's Degree (and specific courses), and finally, passing a comprehensive exam or a series of exams. Another value of pursuing a professional certification is the extensive research and studying of applicable laws, guidance, and policy in your discipline. By obtaining a professional certification, you become an expert in your field. After successfully obtaining my own CGFM certification, I encouraged others to do the same. Many others also followed suit as a result.

Acquiring Knowledge through Personal Experience

Leonardo da Vinci once said, "Wisdom is the daughter of experience."[34] Our past successes, and just as important, our failures are ingrained in who we are and form a substantial part of our knowledge. Every past job or duty assignment bears fruit for future ones as the following story demonstrates.

During one overseas deployment, a young Lieutenant awakened me in my tent. "We have a problem sir," he said. Our host nation had without warning decided to not allow any more of our C-130 cargo and transport aircraft missions to be flown from their country to other locations in the surrounding countries. Their decision to no longer be the operational hub had a significant impact on the Lieutenant and his mission.

As the Disbursing Officer for the entire Southwest Asia area of operations, he operated as the banker, providing cash to other sites, paying bills, and providing guidance to Paying Agents around the region. The Lieutenant and his Paying Agents used the cargo missions to send and receive funds and to turn-in documentation to keep adequate accountability. Occasionally, the Lieutenant would even board a flight to supervise a changeover from one outgoing Paying Agent to the new one. I could tell by his demeanor that he was very worried about providing the necessary support to other bases in the area.

I told the Lieutenant that I had an idea that might work. Using my previous Germany assignment experience, I eventually convinced higher headquarters to relocate our Disbursing Agent operation from the austere location to Ramstein Air Base, Germany. The Lieutenant and his staff now had an operational hub access (planes flying out to the sites), but he also gained access to a superb "financial hub" banking infrastructure in Frankfurt, Germany (wiring funds, obtaining cash, etc). Best of all, the German senior banker (a friend of mine from my previous assignment) considered it part of the existing theater banking agreement and there were no additional service fees.

As a result, we decreased the minimum account balances held in foreign banks from over $10 million to just $1 million – saving taxpayers over half a million dollars annually. As a leader, do not underestimate the power of similar experiences to share with others that we have accumulated or acquired throughout our career.

Acquiring Knowledge through Experience of Others

In his book, *Being George Washington: The Indispensable Man, as You've Never Seen Him*, Glenn Beck describes how one of our greatest presidents used those around him to acquire knowledge.

"Washington's willingness to listen to others, including his subordinates, is what made this possible (Yorktown victory). Being humble means nothing if you don't live it every day. Plenty of bosses, for example, believe themselves to be humble but would never call in a low-level manager or secretary to take their advice about a business deal...but Washington did. He listened to everyone – keeping the good ideas and discarding the bad."[35]

Beck went on to elaborate even more about Washington's desire to learn from others. He wrote, "...throughout his military career Washington frequently met with subordinates and, unlike English commanders, encouraged the free exchange of ideas. He listened more than he talked (one of the rules of civility) and he not only drew from the best ideas of his men, but also credited them generously."[36]

"We all have holes in our knowledge base, and it's important to fill in those holes."[34]

Maria Bartiromo, from the book *The 10 Laws of Enduring Success*

When the Iraq War began in March 2003, I volunteered to be one of the first Air Force Comptrollers to deploy to support

Operation Iraqi Freedom. One of the initial things I did was to reach out to a fellow Comptroller – Major "Dave." Dave had served during the Afghanistan conflict and built a great reputation as a deployed Comptroller

He supported me by sending information that he thought would be helpful to me when I deployed as a Comptroller to Iraq. We talked on the phone and emailed each other frequently leading up to my own deployment. At the very last moment, however, my orders were cancelled and I never did deploy to Iraq. However, I appreciated the willingness of Major Dave to share his own deployment experiences with me. He is now a senior officer in his own right and continues to do great things for our country.

As a leader, when you *LISTEN* to others, you and your followers reap the following benefits:

- **L**earn from others

- **I**nstill pride of ownership

- **S**hare the center stage

- **T**eamwork is promoted

- **E**go is kept in check

- **N**ew ideas are created

Using your own personal experiences to acquire knowledge is important, but inherently limited. Using the *experience of others* adds to the body of knowledge you acquire and then are able to share with others. When you read books such as this one, you are learning by sharing in the lessons learned of another person's experiences, without suffering through the mistakes made along the way.

Using your Leadership Perch

Another means for a leader to acquire knowledge is through the vantage point he or she obtains from their position in the organization hierarchy. By virtue of your position, you are more privy to information at the higher echelons. Be alert to what is happening around you. Stop in and ask your own boss what is going on in their world. This practice adds to your own base of knowledge.

In an excellent article entitled, "A Survival Guide for Leaders," Ronald Heifetz and Marty Linsky raise the importance of a leader to *get off the dance floor and go to the balcony*. The metaphor implies that you have to move from the dance floor (tactical issues) to the balcony (a more strategic "big picture" vantage point), and back to the dance floor on an ongoing basis.[37]

Not everyone has the luxury of a balcony ticket. As a leader in the organization, you do. Take advantage of it by carefully observing the events from your leadership perch and use that knowledge to share with your followers.

Sharing Knowledge

"There is no question that as a leader you have responsibilities to teach. As Major General Perry M. Smith, former Commandant at National War College, says, 'Teachership and leadership go hand-in-glove. The leader must be willing to teach skills, to share insights, and experiences, and to work very closely with people to help them mature and be creative....By teaching, leaders can inspire, motivate, and influence subordinates at various levels'."[38]

General Tony Zinni, from his book *Leading the Charge*

I recall a new assignment to an overseas organization years ago. As I walked around the building, I noticed a bulletin board with a short memorandum posted on it from the person whom I was replacing. He had attended a staff meeting, there were just a few sentences describing the highlights of the meeting and that was it.

He did a poor job of taking advantage of his leadership perch and sharing knowledge as an important form of influence at his disposal. My thought was there was not much of a partnering effort involved in communicating with my future team members.

"Moving toward partnership means eliminating the fear many managers feel about giving up the "power" associated with information. Actually, the "power" they feel they have is often an illusion. The real power lies within the engine – with the people of the organization. It's the leadership's responsibility to empower that engine."[39]

Jim Schaffer, in an article, "Always tell the truth"

Sharing Knowledge as an Important Influence Factor

Recently, my wife Brenda and I went on a nine-day tour of Israel. Our Israeli tourist guide, Shimon, did a fantastic job of explaining the significance of the various venues and sites. He used his extensive tour guide knowledge along with the unique vantage point as a native Jew to share important cultural aspects. In fact, we hope to participate in future tours with Shimon for areas we did not see on this one trip.

Brenda's former professor in religious studies, Dr. Taylor, organized the group trip. He possessed significant influence and credibility as a leader due to his authority (University Dean of Christian Studies and Professor). However, his primary source of power and influence was his ability to share his vast knowledge of the Bible and related doctrine to the group. Dr. Taylor acquired his knowledge through hard work and dedication. He had graduate degrees from the New Orleans Baptist Theological Seminary and a Ph D. from Baylor University. The Professor was also able to *stay ahead of the group* by using his experience in leading pilgrimages to the Holy Land over 20 times.

The group would gather nightly in a hotel conference room

to hear Dr. Taylor put our day's touring into proper context and perspective. He had our undivided attention as we looked to him to answer our many questions about places we visited such as; the Sea of Galilee, the Mount of Beatitudes, Bethlehem, and Jerusalem itself. Besides having the sufficient knowledge that he had acquired through formal education and from his personal experiences visiting Israel, Dr. Taylor was able to share his knowledge with us because we trusted him. All three elements must be in play in order for a leader to share knowledge with a group of his or her followers.

Two Elements build Trust: Competence and Character

"Character is what we are; competence is what we can do. Both character and competence are necessary to inspire trust."[40]

Stephen R. Covey

We can greatly influence our competence when we strive to be the kind of person who is continuously learning. As we have already described earlier in the chapter, there are numerous ways to enhance our knowledge, and therefore our competency, at the same time. They include;

- Formal Education
- Professional Certifications
- Personal Experience
- Experience of Others
- Using your Leadership Perch

As Dr. Covey suggests, however, competency is only one necessary component that leads to trust. The other is character.

Character impacts Trust so that Knowledge is Received

"...people will tend to build a relationship with and follow the person they view as the most trustworthy, who cares the most, and who is willing to always do the right thing."[41]

Coach Tony Dungy, from the book, *The Mentor Leader*

W. Edwards Deming, pioneer of the Quality movement, observed once that, "trust is mandatory for the optimization of any system."   In terms of effectively sharing the knowledge you acquired through various means such as education, professional certifications, and experience, it will do no good if your team is unwilling to receive it. The most likely barrier to receiving your knowledge is a lack of trust. More specifically, trust is lost for a perceived lack of character on the leader's part.

Character should not be on a Learning Curve

While teaching a Leadership course at the Air Force Academy, I was especially mindful that for the senior cadets, they would be entering the "real Air Force" in a short time. Whenever possible, I would apply the course material to situations they would soon be facing as the service's newest officers and leaders.

I emphasized to the class that while they were certainly learning valuable skills at the Academy regarding military training and academics, the challenges facing them on active duty would be more complex and of a different nature.

Fortunately, the vast majority of the Air Force members would recognize that the fresh crop of second lieutenants would ride a *learning curve when it came to job knowledge* in their new careers. I took the liberty of demonstrating the learning curve in a slightly different means to the normal downward slope. The learning curve I developed implies a straight and steep correlation between knowledge and time (figure 2).

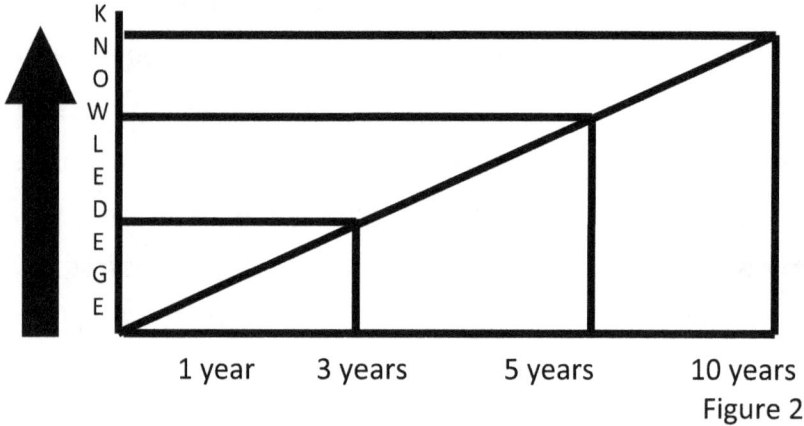

Figure 2

The traditional learning curve is admittedly different. I was emphasizing to the cadets that through time, their knowledge would increase because of experience, additional education, and continuous training. However, I also wanted to make sure they knew that the active duty force would not give them the same slack when it came to their character. Character should not be on a learning curve going from low to high, but on a straight line, *constantly high*, as demonstrated in the second graph (figure 3).

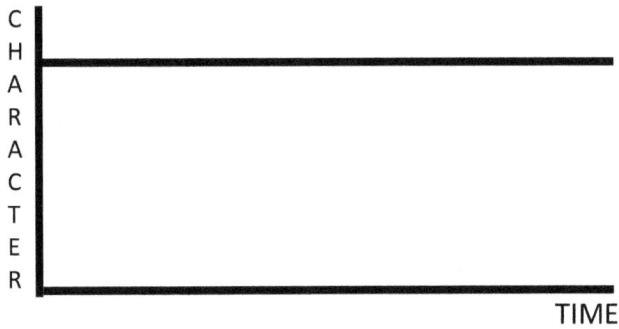

TIME

Figure 3

Some of you may be wondering if my advice to the cadets was realistic. How could young men and women be expected to have a learning curve for job knowledge but maintain a high flat line for character? In reality, my advice ties back to the cornerstone of the Academy way of life, the Cadet Wing Honor Code. The code states:

"We will not lie, steal or cheat, nor tolerate among us anyone who does."[42]

The code does not differentiate between a brand new freshman or a senior ready to graduate and receive a commission as an officer. The character standard is the same for all 4,000 cadets in the Cadet Wing; no lying, no stealing, no cheating, and no tolerance for those who do.

Years later, Secretary of Defense Robert Gates, shared a similar message to another group of future officers, the graduating class of 2011 at the U.S. Naval Academy in Annapolis, Maryland. He gave the following advice on character to the midshipmen:

"Nowadays it seems like integrity – or honor or character – is kind of quaint, a curious, old-fashioned notion...But for a real leader, personal virtues – self-reliance, self-control, honor, truthfulness, morality – are absolute. These are the building blocks of character, of integrity – and only on that foundation can real leadership be built."[43]

Acquiring knowledge will be for naught if your character is questionable to those who need to receive that knowledge. There is a correlation between sharing knowledge and building and holding the trust of your followers. You need to be trusted before others receive your knowledge.

Never use your Knowledge as a Hammer

"Often, we are too slow to recognize how much and in what ways we can assist each other through sharing such expertise and knowledge."[44]

Owen Arthur

Acquiring sufficient knowledge to stay ahead of the group takes an effort on your part and something you should feel good about in obtaining. There are significant sacrifices, in time away from loved ones to go to class or study, financial resources to pay for the training or learning, etc.

One thing a leader should never do is to use your own personal knowledge as a hammer against others when they ask you to share it. Let me explain. If a co-worker or follower tries to tap into your body of knowledge be careful how you respond in kind. Granted, there are two ways of looking at it. The first case is that the person asking the question has not done enough on their part in paying attention to what you already said in the first place. Hall of Fame basketball coach Nancy Lieberman shares an anecdote in her book, *Playbook for Success*, worth repeating:

"When I was coaching in Detroit, I called a time-out just to call a specific play called 'horns.' I diagrammed it, being careful to keep it simple. As the team ran back out on the floor, one player turned around and came back to ask me, 'What are we running?' I was astonished. With this play – that I had *just spelled out* – we would win or lose the game. Yet somehow, she hadn't heard me!"[45]

Coach Lieberman had to repeat to the player what already been shared once with the entire team. She was deservedly frustrated because of the lack of effort in listening.

However, the second case involves a leader who is too quick to anger, or demonstrates impatience, when a follower is seeking feedback from the leader. I have seen leaders who show impatience or frustration and put a dagger into a needed dialogue. If you have ever used the following statements, you may be guilty of using your own knowledge as a hammer on others:

- "I cannot believe you just asked that question."
- "Your remark totally proves that you do not get it."
- "Why in the world would you raise that point?"
- "I already mentioned this before a while back."

A leader should instead *embrace the feedback.* If someone returns back to you 80 percent understanding of the original message; just deal with the other 20 percent *not understood* and be done with it. There is no need to berate somebody, start all over with the initial intent, and pull someone through a knothole unnecessarily. Chances are, if you do, they will not be coming back to you again for guidance or to seek out your knowledge.

In his book, *What Got You Here Won't Get You There*, Marshall Goldsmith shares the following:

"The troublemaking phrase I always look for is, 'I'm confused – because it is so subtle and dishonest. Have you ever had this happen to you? You make a sincere suggestion to your boss, 'Boss, have you ever considered…?' The boss looks at you and says, 'I'm confused by what you're telling me.' The boss doesn't mean he's confused. He's saying *you're confused* – which is another way of saying, 'You're wrong'."[46]

Instead of using cutting questions or comments that use your knowledge as a hammer, try some of the following ones that lead to a healthier dialogue and shared knowledge:

- "Good question, let me try to answer that for you."
- "Excellent point, why do you think that is?"
- "Tell me how you would handle that one?"
- "You're close, but here is the rest of the answer."

Another aspect of this approach is that as we mentioned earlier, leaders acquire knowledge through their own education and experience, but also the experience of others. If a leader uses knowledge as a hammer with others, you are not going to get information that will help you in making the best possible decisions. It is interesting to review Yogi Berra's thoughts on the matter:

"Even when you get older, you should never be a know-it-all. You can always learn from someone else's experiences. When I became a manager, I always listened to the coaches. I figured what's the use of having coaches if you can't use their opinions and experience?"[47]

~~~~~~~~~~
A leader should instead *embrace the feedback*. If someone returns to you 80 percent understanding of the original message; just deal with the 20 percent *not understood* and be done with it.

Final thoughts on Sharing Knowledge

"Please note that sharing information with others is exactly opposite of the way that many leaders mistakenly try to lead. These leaders horde information and refuse to share it with anyone. They seem to think that if they keep information to themselves, they will look smarter than those they want to follow them."[48]

William A. Cohen, *The Art of the Leader*

A leader has a "handful" of influences and power available to use. Each of them is as individual as the fingers on our hand, but in combination are a powerful force. In the rewards chapter, epitomized as using your thumb, a leader is encouraged to offer followers *cake and a break*, representing rewards and an opportunity.

In the same manner, a leader is encouraged to freely give and share from the knowledge acquired over a lifetime of learning. Our index finger, symbolic of possessing an "aha" moment when pointed to our brain, represents *knowledge* in our talk to the hand leadership concept.

The index finger has several dimensions in its use. You can use it playfully and innocently to point to someone in a friendly gesture. Think of politicians on a stage when they point to someone they recognize in the audience. They are usually smiling at the same time, and the motion is a positive signal.

Conversely, an index finger could also be used to single someone out in a negative manner. From the witness box, a person identifies the suspected criminal by pointing to them, as instructed by the prosecutor.

Use your knowledge, whenever possible, in a constructive manner (the way rewards are used) to lift up your followers and not as a hammer against them. As the Apostle Paul said, "Knowledge puffs up....The man who thinks he knows something does not yet know as he ought to know." Sharing knowledge improves ability, and sharing rewards can improve motivation. Together, both can improve individual and organizational performance.

Assume the Talk to the Hand position with your right hand (palm facing out) extending at eye level as Brenda does on the book cover. Now clench your fingers into a fist. Next, point your index finger straight up and then point your thumb sidewise to the left. Remember, the index finger represents sharing knowledge and the thumb represents use of rewards.

A person facing your hand would see that you just made the sign language for the letter "L" –as in Leadership.

We could probably stop right here, with the thumb and index fingers (representing rewards and knowledge respectively) and still come out ahead leading people. However, let us continue talking to the hand. In the next several chapters, we move to fingers that represent discipline and authority. We will see that these factors are certainly not as *positive* to followers as rewards and knowledge. Nevertheless, they are important influence factors for a leader to use. These factors are used sparingly compared to the "thumbs up" for rewards or pointing to the brain for knowledge. At the right time, however, they provide the necessary *balance* you need to be an even more effective leader.

Chapter Five

Middle Finger: Punish Wisely

~~~~~~~~~~

Our longest finger can do the most damage.

When I joined the Air Force right out of high school, my first assignment was at Lackland Air Force Base, Texas for basic training. All the Training Instructors were imposing figures but I remember one in particular. He was big, tall, and mean. This one particular Sergeant had a habit of getting in your face and poking at your chest with his middle finger. I have to admit that it probably felt like a jackhammer beating into my chest mainly because of the dramatic effect of him doing so.

In various cultures, the middle finger of course represents an obscene gesture – let us just say the *opposite of giving out rewards*. In our Talk to the Hand Leadership Concept, the middle finger represents use of discipline or punishment.

Potential Consequences when using Punishment

"Punishment cannot heal spirits, can only break them."[49]

Barbara Deming

Of all the forms of influence available in the Talk to the Hand leadership tool, punishment (analogous to the middle finger) is one that warrants the most caution in using. Notice on your hand, that for most people, the middle finger sticks out the longest (not the index finger). Try to remember it this way. *Our longest finger can do the most damage.*

Let us take a moment to review the *impact* of punishment when compared to the other fingers on our hand (figure 4):

Thumb	-	Rewards	-	Positive Impact
Pinky	-	Relationship	-	Positive Impact
Index Finger	-	Knowledge	-	Primarily Positive
Ring Finger	-	Authority	-	Positive *or* Negative
Middle Finger	-	**Punishment**	-	**Negative Impact**

Some will contend that punishment itself can lead to proper behavior by defining boundaries, etc, and I do not argue that point. My aim is to emphasize that of the five elements of leadership influence, punishment is the one with a solely negative impact at the time that it is given.

Figure 4

> ~~~~~~~~~~
> The whole point of the Talk to the Hand
> Concept is for a leader to be aware of what
> power is available (fingers), and proper
> discernment in which one to use.

Early in my career, I once worked for a Colonel who unfortunately, tended to lose his temper, sometimes in public. On one occasion, there was a problem in one of the sections so I scheduled a meeting directly with the workers involved – without the immediate supervisor. I felt that the group would be more likely to speak freely and honestly without their boss in the same room.

The Colonel's office was right next to the conference room where I was conducting the meeting, and in the middle of it, his secretary interrupted to say that the Colonel wanted to see me. I informed her that I would do so after the meeting. She told me that he meant "now" as in immediately. I apologized to the group and walked in to see the Colonel in his office.

He was literally red in the face with anger and began to scream at me that I should *never* conduct a meeting in that manner without the supervisor in the room. He questioned my ability as an officer and leader and continued to berate me for about 15 minutes.

The Colonel used the wrong set of power and influence at his disposal. He should have used the situation as a *teaching moment.* As an experienced and high-ranking officer, he could have *shared his knowledge* and explained to me the rationale behind his advice. If he wanted to emphasize his point by being firm, that would be okay too. However, there was *no sharing of knowledge*, a seasoned Colonel could have passed to a young Lieutenant willing to listen and learn. In reflection, I actually see his point about honoring the chain of command in the manner that I expected it from my own supervisors. Back then, however, when I left the room, I remembered only one thing – my boss acting mad and yelling, and not much beyond that.

The whole point of the Talk to the Hand Concept is for a leader to be aware of what power is available (fingers), and proper discernment in which one to use. In short, the Colonel used the wrong finger – middle (punishment) instead of index finger (sharing knowledge). Ironically, the Colonel's boorish behavior and temper caught up with him and he was forced to retire from the Air Force.

Potential Consequences when choosing *not* to Punish

"Rewarding the positive takes effort, but it is pretty easy to do. Confronting negative behavior is tougher...But when a person's behavior is inappropriate, *avoiding confrontation always worsens the situation*."[50]

John Maxwell, renowned leadership expert

In the same manner, a leader can do damage by inappropriately administering punishment, there can also be damage if choosing to *not* discipline when the situation calls for it. Just as a child needs boundaries, an organization needs them too. If unacceptable behavior goes unchecked, you are only creating confusion and poor morale in the workplace.

Recall what we discussed in the Rewards chapter earlier: A tangible reward is important because the followers offered something *tangibly positive* to earn the incentive in the first place. In this case, discipline or punishment is important because the followers demonstrated something *tangibly negative* to warrant the punishment.

The *Beyond a Reasonable Doubt* Discipline Rule

After describing the negative consequences of choosing to punish perhaps too quickly, and then the ramifications if you choose not to, you may become hesitant on which way to go. A tool that I developed years ago that I would like to share with you is called The Beyond a Reasonable Doubt (BARD) Discipline Rule.

We are all familiar with the legal term, beyond a reasonable doubt. A judge advises jury members to hear and weigh the evidence, and reach a conclusion of not guilty or guilty that is beyond a reasonable doubt. A *reasonable doubt* arises from a logical thought process by judging the evidence presented to the alleged offense (i.e., not based on sympathy). Beyond a reasonable doubt is a very high standard, not based on absolute certainty.

You can use the beyond a reasonable doubt (BARD)

discipline rule as a simple, yet powerful guide in determining when to discipline. The rule goes like this:

The BARD Discipline Rule
Never discipline your people unless you are
beyond a reasonable doubt they deserve it.

The BARD discipline rule accomplishes two very important outcomes. First, you keep your credibility high by not overreacting too quickly. Second, when the evidence warrants it, you have no choice but to act accordingly.

By not scolding or disciplining your people
until you research the matter, you will
find that a vast majority of the time, your
staff was right or innocent.

Cruel and Unusual Punishment

After weighing all the circumstances, if you decide that someone is beyond a reasonable doubt in requiring discipline, you still must be careful not to go overboard in the punishment itself.

The punishment should fit the discretion involved.

As an Air Force squadron commander, I had the benefit of counsel of the staff judge advocate when deciding on the appropriate punishment of a military member. The base lawyers served as effective *levelers of justice*. What we did not need is someone who was too extreme in their punishment, nor someone who was too lenient either. The legal staff, therefore, could recommend to a commander facing a situation, the "standard" penalty for the offense.

The form or type of discipline or punishment should vary with the severity of the action. Be careful in this regard. You may be restricted on the discipline based on company policy. Consult your Human Resources staff for guidance and counsel after you have had a chance to look at all the available options. When possible, try to deal with the disciplinary matter in an escalating manner, and at the lowest level.

Part of being a good leader is discernment in making tough decisions involving people. Just as becoming angry too quickly can damage a leader's reputation, administering excessive, or cruel and unusual punishment, will do similar damage.

Benefit of the Doubt

In most circumstances, your people will do their best and try to achieve good results. That philosophy should be your guiding principle. In my experience, rarely will someone go out of their way to deliberately do something wrong. Today's fast-paced environment may drive an honest mistake or two. Consider that inevitability before imposing any punishment or discipline. I am certain that we have made a few honest mistakes in our own careers, and appreciated the boss giving *us* benefit of the doubt.

In a *Harvard Business Review* article entitled, "Strategies for Learning from Failure," Amy Edmondson proposes a *spectrum* of reasons for failure. Deliberate deviance is first on the list and warrants blame (and probably punishment). A lack of effort could be next on the list and so on across the spectrum.[51]

When Edmonson asked executives to determine how many failures are truly blameworthy, surprisingly the normal response was in the 2 to 5 percent range. However, when asked how many times mistakes or failures are *treated* as blameworthy, the percentage was between 70 to 90 percent.[52]

The forces around you that might explain this difference include customers, suppliers, your own boss, stakeholders, and the demands and challenges of our technological explosion. For example, dealing with other departments or customers can sometimes create perceived mistakes from your workforce that may not be true at all.

Before jumping to conclusions, gather the facts and weigh the evidence. I have found that there are always two sides of the story. I contend that you can probably find two sides to every two sides of the story.

By not scolding or disciplining your people until you research the matter, you will find that a vast majority of the time, your staff was right or innocent. Sometimes, it is your own lack of direction, or unclear communication on your part, that may cause a problem. In short, look at your own part in the equation before acting to discipline others.

A Time to Take Action

There will be times, when upon gathering all the facts and weighing the evidence, you must hold your people accountable. I am not talking about that honest mistake that comes from lack of training or pressures on the job. These errors will happen routinely.

The circumstances that warrant discipline or punishment are more severe than honest mistakes. They include lying, stealing disrupting the workplace, sexual harassment, discrimination, insubordination, etc. These types of negative acts must not be overlooked.

Presidential examples of using the BARD Rule

During the Civil War, President Lincoln needed victories in the battlefield to meet his primary objective of preserving the Union. He supported and encouraged his Generals by frequently writing or visiting them in the field. Lincoln, in particular, had a high regard for General Ulysses Grant who without fanfare or concern for rank, garnered him much needed victories.

Lincoln did not have the same good fortune with other

Generals on his staff. When rumors of Grant's fondness of alcohol reached Lincoln, he concluded after investigating it that his drinking did not impair his ability to plot and execute wartime strategy. In fact, Lincoln halfway seriously joked that if he could find the brand of whiskey Grant was drinking he would distribute it to all of his Generals.[53]

Another General besides Grant started with a positive impression on Lincoln. In July 1861, General George McClellan rode into Washington, D.C. to take command of the Army of the Potomac as a handsome, athletic, 34-year old ready to in his own words, become the "power of the land."[54] Initially, McClellan was able to pass his self-confidence to his demoralized troops. Lincoln felt that he finally had a winner after previous failures in the commander of the Army of the Potomac.

Unfortunately, McClellan talked a better game than actually delivering results. Further, his arrogance often led to open disdain for the President and even leaving Lincoln in his downstairs parlor while he passed word that he was retiring for the evening. After several visits and personal letters, Lincoln gave the young General still another chance. In a telegraph that amounts to a direct order, Lincoln conveyed to McClellan: "....directs you that you cross the Potomac and give battle to the enemy or drive him south. Your army must move now while the roads are good."[55]

In response, McClellan offered only his regular menu of excuses why he could not take the fight to the enemy. Finally, Lincoln had enough of the man of once he famously said, "He's got the slows."

Using our Beyond a Reasonable Doubt rule for discipline, Lincoln did the right thing in hindsight. The President was certainly patient (some would say almost to a fault) with McClellan and did not act hastily. He gave him the benefit of the doubt, especially early on. Lincoln's own role in the matter was clean. He did not ask anything unreasonable or unrealistic of his commander and he provided him the adequate resources to get the job done. Lincoln had to deal with the McClellan situation on two counts: growing insubordination and inaction.

In our BARD rule, Lincoln was absolutely justified to discipline the wayward commander, and fire him from his role as Commander of the Army of the Potomac.

Almost a century later, another President had to deal with another General with an oversized ego. In this case, however, this General was overly aggressive in the field. When North Korea crossed the 38th parallel into South Korea in June 1950, the country turned to one of its most respected war heroes, General Douglas MacArthur to lead the response.

Within three months, MacArthur crafted the historic landing at Inchon which turned the tide of the war and forced the North Koreans to retreat back across the 38th parallel that separated both countries. It was a brilliant military move and MacArthur, already popular from World War II successes, gained even further celebrity status.[56]

President Truman repeatedly sought assurances from MacArthur to do nothing that would provoke China and Russia to join the Korean Conflict. The General reassured the President that would not be the case. Only two months after the invasion, the Chinese did engage, sending over a quarter of a million troops into Korea, forcing MacArthur to retreat.[57]

While the President sought a peaceful solution to the situation, MacArthur continuously pressed him to take the fight to the Chinese. MacArthur, like McClellan with Lincoln, did not hide his displeasure with the President and even did so through the media. MacArthur was digging a deeper hole for himself by his increasingly insubordinate actions.[58]

Finally, the last straw came when MacArthur personally issued an ultimate directly to the Chinese to surrender or face dire military consequences. In fact, Truman sought the opposite – peace. President Truman had enough and waited a bit longer to gain consensus from the military brass that MacArthur must be fired for his blatant insubordination.[59]

The BARD discipline rule in this case demanded action. In his book, *Presidential Leadership: 15 Decisions That Changed the Nation,* Nick Ragone noted the following:

"In some respects, Truman's decision to fire MacArthur was an easy one: no general could survive multiple acts of insubordination, and this was no exception. Truman believed it was important for military leaders to respect civilian authority. Allowing MacArthur to get away with blatant insubordination sent the wrong signal."[60]

Whether a President, a shop supervisor, or schoolteacher, we all face difficult decisions when it comes to discipline and punishment. Think clearly and assess each situation. As we noted earlier, there may be only a small percentage of time, when a follower is blameworthy for material and conscious discretions versus honest mistakes. When that time comes, however, a leader must act decisively.

> ~~~~~~~~~~~
> A leader makes tough calls all the time, especially when it comes to correcting people's missteps. For some supervisors, it is one of the toughest decisions to make.

On the Receiving End of my own Rule

Let me share a story where I deserved to be on the receiving end of the BARD discipline rule. During one assignment, part of my duties was to support a network of reserve officers. These officers recruited high school students to attend the Air Force Academy on a part-time basis. They are a great group of dedicated patriots and I enjoyed working with them. Many had full-time jobs as airline pilots, lawyers, business owners, etc, and were model citizens.

There was an administrative side of my job in addition to actually managing their recruiting efforts. I reviewed all their annual performance reports for example. A well-written annual appraisal is a key component of a promotion package and I did my best to ensure a fair and accurate report for each individual officer.

One particular performance appraisal came to my desk for a review. In this case, I knew the officer because we worked together on a few projects and I thought the report in front of me did not properly reflect the person's achievements. In short, the report demonstrated a poor effort on the writer's part. After a few phone calls and emails with the responsible Director, I decided that I would personally work on the report myself to improve the quality before sending it over as a final product.

My good intentions soon backfired however when my own boss received a complaint that I was "holding up" the processing of the report from my end. Events were turning in the wrong direction I had anticipated.

One morning, my supervisor came up to me, and without his customary morning greeting, pressed me if the report was processed. I tried to explain the background and circumstances to him but he curtly directed me to get it done today. I went back to my office and stewed a bit.

I thought, "How could he do that?" Here I was, trying to do the right thing, and I got chewed out over it. I drafted a brief note and put it on top of the finished report along with copies of the email traffic with the Director in the field. I walked over to my supervisor's office to discuss it some more but he was not there. I decided to leave the report and the rest of the package on top of his desk.

Later that day, my boss came by my desk to tell me would like to speak to me. When I arrived at his office, he asked me to close the door behind me and take a seat. Here is a revelation: When the boss asks you to close the door and sit down, it probably is *not* a good thing. My supervisor achieved the rank of full Colonel in the Air Force, and was a former fighter pilot. He proceeded to inform me that he was disappointed about my "in your face" attitude over this performance report. He told me that this type of behavior did not reflect my normal professionalism, and he wanted me to straighten up and get over this episode.

In my warped mind, I had actually been expecting an apology from him instead of a reprimand. I thought to myself, he obviously did not read the email traffic I had provided him. After all, I just wanted the performance report to be a good one.

In reflection, my boss was right in his own actions. Remember, the BARD rule says, "Never discipline your people until you are beyond a reasonable doubt it is deserved." In my case, I had clearly crossed the line with my insubordinate response. Instead of making a production about his initial inquiry, I could have said something like, "Yes sir, I will take care of that performance report right away." What was wrong with that statement? Could it be my own ego was in the way of not admitting a mistake on my part – not getting it done on my end because of my own procrastination?

If I had told my boss I would take care of it when he asked me, he most likely would have said "thanks," and moved on. Instead, I tried to rationalize my own poor behavior with my good intentions. My attitude deserved to be disciplined, plain and simple. The boss needed to deal with it. The BARD discipline rule demanded action – and he took it.

In my case, being in the military at the time, my high-ranking boss had a full range of discipline actions at his disposal. He could have given me a formal reprimand or a letter of admonishment. If he did, it could have been a career killer for me. The Colonel was a good boss, and a good man. He did not go overboard and administer any cruel or unusual punishment. His discipline was to "call me on the carpet," and tell me in very clear terms, that I was wrong and he did not expect similar behavior in the future. It was enough to capture my attention because I did not cross that line with him again.

A leader makes tough calls all the time, especially when it comes to correcting people's missteps. For some supervisors, it is one of the toughest decisions to make. Yet, if you do not take firm disciplinary action, it is wrong for many reasons. In my case, it was not just the performance report timeliness as the primary issue; it was preserving good order and discipline.

By correcting me, he placed the mission ahead of my personal concerns, the right move. How many times do you see a supervisor catering to people by listening to their whining? It is called appeasement. As much as you may hate to discipline your people, when called for, you must do so. If you do not, you are hurting your mission, but also your people and yourself at the same time.

Imagine if my boss took no action at my disrespectful

behavior. Suppose he agreed with me that, it was a poor report in the first place and not my problem. The Director in the field should have done a better job. When the subject of timely performance reports came up among the rest of my peers, I may have told them do not worry, it was no big deal to the boss.

> ~~~~~~~~~~
> The BARD discipline rule in effect slows you down and forces you to catch your breath first. At the same time, the BARD rule also moves you to take decisive action when there is a need to do so as my boss did with me.

Discipline in the Desert

While deployed for six months in Saudi Arabia, I used the BARD discipline rule on one of my favorite troops. "Nick" was a sharp Non-Commissioned Officer (NCO) with a great attitude, and he worked hard and effectively in our office. During a short time period, however, he abused our privilege of a weekly personal phone call to stay in touch with those back home. He also lost the office key that each of us had been issued upon arrival. You might be asking yourself, "What is the big deal? It is only a key and a phone call?"

In the deployed situation, we looked forward to our one phone call every week that we were allowed to make back to the United States. To be fair to everyone on the installation, we were told to keep our calls to 15 minutes. Sure, sometimes we were caught up in a conversation and busted the timeline by a minute or so. Nick had done so too many times and way beyond reasonable timelines. In addition, by losing his office key, it placed our own personal safety at risk.

Only a few years earlier, 19 U.S. Air Force members and one Saudi employee were killed as a result of a terrorist bombing at the Khobar Towers housing complex. Additionally, nearly 400 people of other nationalities were wounded. In order to improve our Force Protection, the 4404th Provisional Wing was relocated to the Prince Sultan Air Base, Saudi Arabia. Because of our history with terrorism, losing an office key was considered a significant breach to our personal safety and security.

I was upset with Nick for putting his teammates at a security risk for carelessness on his part. In addition, by abusing *his* phone privileges, the commander could have made an example out of our entire unit and we all could have lost our ability to stay in touch back home.

I drafted up a letter of admonishment and had Nick formally report in to me with the ranking NCO also present. He stood at attention while I slowly read him the punishment. He signed the letter and readily acknowledged his mistakes. If he failed again on either count, the next set of consequences would escalate proportionately.

A day or two later, Nick came back and asked me if it would be all right to use that same letter as an example of discipline when he needed to impose it on others. Nick was aspiring to become an officer himself and he knew the value of fair and evenhanded discipline. He was given me feedback that my punishment was the right call and in the right manner.

I stayed in touch him with for numerous years and I am proud to report that Nick is an outstanding Air Force Intelligence Officer now serving his country with distinction. The BARD discipline rule is a valuable tool for any supervisor to use.

Seek Consistency when Punishing

"A lot of women (and men) resist confrontation. They'll do almost anything to avoid sitting down with someone face-to-face to make a bad situation right. In such circumstances, resist the temptation to react in a knee-jerk, overly emotional way, especially if you are mad; instead, take time to contemplate, to cool down."[61]

Coach Nancy Lieberman, from her book *Playbook for Success*

The real value of using the BARD discipline rule is that it keeps your actions consistent. As that great American Yogi Berra once noted: "I don't want to make the same mistake twice." You should not discipline your people merely because you are having a bad day or have a temper problem. The BARD discipline rule in effect slows you down and forces you to catch your breath first. At the same time, the BARD rule also moves you to take decisive action when there is a need to do so as my boss did with me.

Final thoughts on use of Punishment

"Anyone can become angry – that is easy, but to be angry with the right person, to the right degree, at the right time, for the right purpose, and in the right way – this is not easy."[62]

Aristotle

Being able to channel our anger constructively is not an easy thing to do, as Aristotle alludes to above, and I have been guilty myself of misuse. As an Adjunct instructor at the Air Force Academy, I remember one incident that I am not proud of that involved cadet students in my upper-division Leadership course. I had assigned to them a project to review a Training Guide for the various volunteer positions available to those assigned to the Academy. For example, each of the 40 cadet squadrons was run by a full-time Air Officer Commanding (AOC), normally a Captain or a Major. To assist them, other positions were available such as Associate AOC, Student Training Officer, etc. At the time, my primary duties involved military training and I had written the guide to assist the volunteers perform their duties. I sought cadet feedback to the guide to get their perspective before we went final with it to see if it captured the necessary functions for each of the positions.

When I handed out the guide to my students, I assigned a suspense date to return the draft with their comments and suggestions for improvement. The morning that the "assignment" was due, the cadets turned in their reviews on the way out the door when the period had officially ended. As frequently occurs, I engaged in a conversation with one or two of the students and did not notice who had or had not turned in their assignments.

Several days later, as class began two students came up to me with the draft study guide and apologized for being late. I took offense to them missing the deadline and did something I now see as completely over-the-top. I threw their reviews in the trash can and told both of them to wait for me in the cafeteria downstairs until the end of the class where I would go down to meet with them.

When I did meet with the cadets about an hour later, I had regained my composure. I was able to stress to them the importance of meeting deadlines. They would soon be entering active duty as second lieutenants, and I emphasized that time management skills and meeting expectations of the boss were very important. Both cadets were very gracious and conveyed they understood my message, and again, apologized for being late. It was during this time together that I adequately used the event as a proper and important teaching moment.

Yet, in hindsight, I violated several of my own rules when it came to discipline. Note: I had not developed them at the time of this incident. First, I had played a part in the scenario in the first place. Was it fair to use the cadets to provide feedback to my own job-related work? The assignment was not part of the formal syllabus and not even graded. In hindsight, I had overstepped by boundaries and misused my authority as an Adjunct instructor.

Second, the BARD, or Beyond a Reasonable Doubt discipline rule, states that a leader should count to ten, take a deep breath, and gather all the facts before dishing out any punishment or discipline. I did not do that when I reacted too quickly at the beginning of class. I should have calmly said that I would like to see both of them after class to discuss it further. It still would have sent a signal to them and the entire class that I was not letting their lateness go without probing further into the matter. Coach Tony Dungy has the right idea in this matter as he relayed it to his new team (from his book, *Quiet Strength*).

He recalled his message: "When I get mad," I continued, "I usually talk at the same volume I'm talking now. And when I get really mad" – I paused –"I *whisper*. So if my voice at this level won't get your attention, and you believe you need someone to yell at you to correct you or motivate you, then we'll probably need to find you another team to play for so that you can play your best."[63]

During my own corrective incident with the cadets, I dishonored a cardinal rule when I punished them in front of others instead of doing so privately. I even violated the cruel and unusual punishment tenet when I threw their assignments into the trashcan and dismissed them from the classroom. Frankly, that behavior was rude and excessive on my part and caused them unwarranted embarrassment in front of their peers. The only good news is that in the end, I did share my knowledge from my many years of active duty experience that being on time was an important trait.

However, before then, I had misused my authority and discipline influences in a negative manner. I had done to the cadets what I mentioned earlier what my Colonel boss did to me when he yelled at me for speaking to subordinates without their supervisor being present.

As stated in the beginning of this chapter, the middle finger – being the longest – can do the most damage. Like fire, it can be helpful and has its purpose, but it can also burn you and others if you are not careful with it. As an ancient Chinese proverb states: "The superior man is clear-minded and cautious in imposing penalties." Therefore, always use discernment when punishing others.

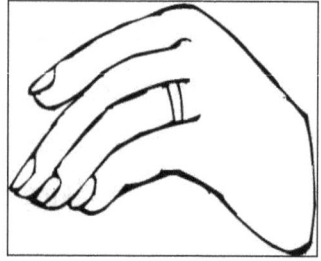

Chapter Six

Ring Finger: Using your Status and Authority

"Entering into a marriage changes the legal status of both parties and gives both husband and wife new rights and obligations."[64]

Cornell University Law School

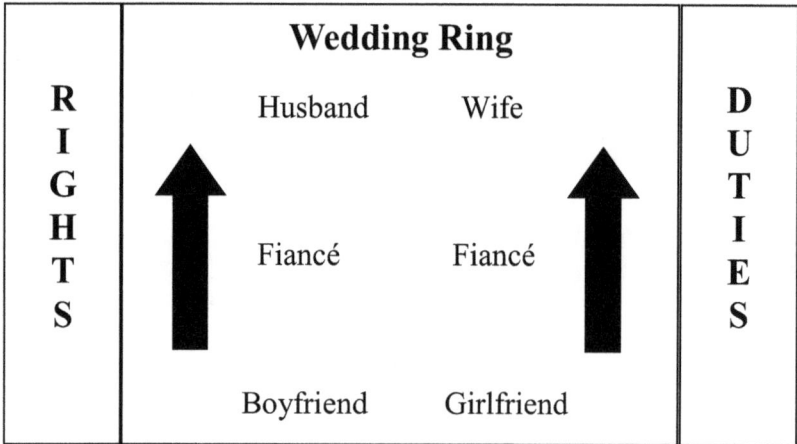

R I G H T S		**Wedding Ring**		D U T I E S
		Husband	Wife	
	↑	Fiancé	Fiancé	↑
		Boyfriend	Girlfriend	

For most of us, a relationship between two people evolves over time. We may start as just friends or casual acquaintances. Next, the pair becomes boyfriend and girlfriend and makes introductions to others in that way. If the relationship continues going well, there is a more formal commitment that leads to engagement status. When two people exchange vows and a wedding ring, the legal status of that relationship changes forever. At that point, a marriage can only be terminated by a court granting a divorce (or an annulment) [65]

In our Talk to the Hand Leadership Concept, we use the ring finger to represent that a leader possesses authority by virtue of their position or corporate rank obtained over time. An individual may start off as an employee on the lower rung and begin to work their way up by virtue of job performance, experience, education, awards, -- a track record. As in the personal relationship, rights and responsibilities evolve over time between the firm and the employee who enters the managerial ranks.

It is through *authority* that a manager can issue rewards, or if necessary, administer punishment to their followers. A wise leader uses authority judiciously, not overemphasizing it as the only form of influence. At the same time, a leader should not give away his or her authority, because doing so only diminishes their ability to influence others.

A leader has three objectives when it comes to authority:

- Use for benefit of the organization and others

- To *draw the line* for inappropriate behavior

- Not give away too easily

Using your Status and Authority Selflessly

"Never let your ego get so close to your position that when your position goes, your ego goes with it."[66]

General Colin Powell

> ~~~~~~~~~~
> A leader should balance the *benefits* received due to command with the *requirements* of command. Striving for wisdom in leadership is the first objective.

In the military, a change-of-command ceremony is a special event where the organization gathers to bid farewell to an outgoing commander and to welcome onboard a new one. The ceremony is steep in military tradition. I was fortunate to not only attend many of these ceremonies as a spectator, but on two occasions, as an active participant as a commander. Assuming command, with all its inherent responsibility and authority, is a special moment in a military person's career and a treasured moment to cherish.

During many of the change-of-command ceremonies, an installation chaplain is part of the event, and often will use the following words from Luke 12:48: "For everyone to whom much is given, of him shall much be required."

An incoming commander is given many things; authority of

the members under his or her command, depending on rank level, escalating punishment authority, or conversely, the ability to promote. A commander is a respected person both within the unit, and externally, to fellow commanders and senior leadership as a key member of the team. Perks such as an organizational flag, a nice office, administrative support, budget authority, etc, are part of command responsibilities.

A leader should balance the *benefits* received due to command with the *requirements* of command. Striving for wisdom in leadership is the first objective.

> Give therefore Thy servant an understanding heart to judge Thy people, that I may discern between good and bad, for who is able to judge this Thy so great a people?
>
> I Kings: 3:9

The Wisdom of Solomon

"Oh, Thou God that heard Solomon in the night when he prayed for wisdom, hear me," Lincoln prayed. "I cannot lead this people: I cannot guide the affairs of this nation without thy help. I am poor and weak and sinful. Oh God, Who didst hear Solomon when he cried for wisdom, hear me and save this nation."[67]

From the book, *The Leadership Wisdom of Solomon*, by Pat Williams

Pat Williams is a senior vice-president of the Orlando Magic basketball team organization, a former coach himself, and ranks among the country's most notable speakers and authors. I once heard him speak at a conference in Orlando, Florida and sent him a note and copy of my book *The Leader's Pyramid: a balanced and consistent approach to leadership*. Pat was gracious enough to respond with an autographed copy of one of his books, *The Winning Combination: 21 keys to Coaching and Leadership Greatness*.

In one of his most recent books, *The Leadership Wisdom of Solomon*, Coach Williams described another situation where one of our Presidents invoked Solomon as a model leader. Harry S. Truman had been on the job less than one hundred days as the new Vice-President to the popular and successful President Franklin Delano Roosevelt when FDR died suddenly. The nation, in the throngs of World War II, looked to the new leader as Israel had looked to Solomon when he replaced their beloved King David.[68] Before a joint session of Congress, Truman said the following, "As I have assumed my duties, I humbly pray Almighty God, in the words of King Solomon: 'Give therefore Thy servant an understanding heart to judge Thy people, that I may discern between good and bad, for who is able to judge this Thy so great a people?' I ask only to be a good and faithful servant of my Lord and my people."[69]

Williams goes on to suggest key strategies for a leader to lead with the wisdom of Solomon. Among them, they include:[70]

Vision – Solomon envisioned an Israel that was expansive (to protect its borders), ample commerce, and prosperous

Communication skills – Solomon could inspire through words

People skills – He forged alliances with external leaders and rallied his own people to work together

Good character – Solomon's exemplary character led to trust and support

Competence – He was a learned and accomplished

Boldness – His bold construction projects and ambitious trade practices put his vision into action

Servanthood – Solomon felt he should serve God and his people

Use your Status and Authority to Draw the Line in the Sand

In the book, *The Bible on Leadership*, author Lorin Woolfe describes a situation where four African-Americans approached a manager (white) about the lack of opportunity for advancement (we described as a "break" earlier), and racially insensitive jokes in the workplace. In order to get smarter on the matter, the manager attended a race relations course.[71]

Ironically, he faced similar hostilities at the race relations course itself, but this time as a white-person "minority." The manager came back more committed than ever to change the culture back in his workplace. He rocked the boat by pushing hard for gender and racial equality in hiring and promotion practices. When he became the executive in charge of a subsidiary company, he continued these policies and not surprisingly, turned a business profit along the way.[72]

A new leader should emphasize certain non-negotiable lines in the sand early and often. Clearly and forcefully, spell out a zero tolerance for any discrimination (racial, gender, etc) or off-color jokes. Similarly, draw another line for any sexual harassment or innuendos. Continue to re-draw these lines because over time they can become less clear. By drawing a line in the sand in these areas, hopefully you minimize the occasions you need to use discipline or punishment when someone decides to cross over the line. Invariably, someone crosses it and you must act decisively to set the proper tone in the organization.

The Importance of Celebrating Special Observances

> The real benefit of promoting diversity, whether gender, ethnicity, religion, etc, is to allow all to participate so that all can contribute. Leaders cannot consider themselves a total leader unless they lead all of their people to common objectives.

You can use your authority to draw the line for inappropriate behavior such as discrimination or harassment in the workplace by fully supporting special observances throughout the year. The main purpose of observing events like African-American Heritage or Hispanic-American Heritage Month is to combat any negative stereotypes that still exist in our society.

For example, Hispanics make up approximately 16 percent of the U.S. population (nearly 1 in 6). Yet, they make up only two or three percent of the characters shown on television shows or in news related stories (1 in 40 proportion). The rare times that Hispanics are featured, two-thirds of the time it is negative in nature: illegal immigration, terrorism, crime, drugs, only able to perform manual labor, uneducated, heavy accents, etc.

If a man from Mars landed in your backyard while you were sleeping, and grabbed the remote and started flipping through channels, he would think there were very few Hispanics and they did not contribute much benefit to our society. Perhaps the man from Mars is not influenced by this misguided characterization, but our children and grandchildren likely will be.

My wife Brenda is an attractive, blue-eyed blonde (she is on the front cover of the book) from North Carolina. The first day she reported to a new middle school teaching assignment in Mobile, Alabama she was asked about her nameplate by her students. The students in typical junior-high fashion, asked her,"What's up with that?" She replied to them, "Garcia, yes that is my married name. My husband is Hispanic." After a short pause, one of them merely asked, "Oh, is he an illegal alien?" I guess I should feel fortunate that they did not ask if I was a terrorist or dealing drugs too.

The point is that there are similar stereotypes for numerous groups of people that still exist in our society that need to be addressed. A leader *should stay ahead of the group* in this area as well by wholeheartedly promoting special observances to combat negative stereotypes and promote diversity as a positive force – not a negative one.

I give great credit to Mr. Gil Jamieson, the person in charge of the FEMA Katrina recovery efforts, headquartered in our New Orleans office, for promoting special observances in the Gulf Coast. Although I reported directly to the FEMA Chief Financial Officer in Washington, DC, I was also a key member of Gil's staff and supported his vision and strategy.

Shortly after reporting in, I volunteered to be a speaker for Hispanic Heritage Month. We formed a small committee of volunteers and put together a nice event for the New Orleans-based workforce. Keep in mind, for the majority of disasters that FEMA provided support to state and local governments, the emphasis is more short-term in nature and response driven. Who had time to worry about a special observance month? With Hurricane Katrina, we were going to be there for long-term recovery, five years and beyond.

In my mind, this meant that the practices encouraged for most federal departments and agencies applied to us as well. As the Katrina CFO, I encouraged such events as part of doing recovery business. I set a very conservative budget of between $500 to $1,000 for each of the various recovery offices in the Gulf Coast – a real bargain and return on investment as far as I was concerned.

When Gil heard of what we had done for Hispanic Heritage month in the New Orleans office, he encouraged me to speak at all the recovery offices. I drove to our locations in Baton Rouge, Louisiana, Biloxi, Mississippi, Montgomery, Alabama, and the only venue I needed to take a commercial flight, Texas. Mr. Jamieson encouraged all his state Directors to get behind the initiative and they certainly did so with gusto.

We then built on this initial momentum and continued with other observances including the African-American Heritage Month a few months later. I invited my good friend and mentor L.C. Williams (mentioned in an earlier chapter) to speak to us in New Orleans and he even did so at his own expense, refusing to take any federal funding for his travel expenses. L.C. is a great speaker and he gave a rousing speech that inspired the many people in attendance.

Leaders like L.C. and Gil use their authority for the benefit of others. Promoting the value of diversity in the workplace through special observance months is one way a leader can leverage that authority. The real benefit of promoting diversity, whether gender, ethnicity, religion, etc, is to allow all to participate so that all can contribute. Leaders cannot consider themselves a total leader unless they lead all of their people to common objectives.

My Experience in Drawing a Line in the Sand

> ~~~~~~~~~
> You need to use your authority to draw, and
> sometimes re-draw, the line in the sand
> because if you are normally gregarious, the
> line invariably becomes *less clear* over time.

By nature, I am a "people person," who enjoys motivating and mentoring those around me. The fingers (forms of power and influence) that come naturally to me, are the thumb (using rewards), the index finger (sharing knowledge), and the pinky finger (forging a good personal relationship). As a result, these are my preferred forms of influence.

However, I have learned that the other two fingers, middle (discipline) and ring (authority) must also be used at the right time. Fortunately, you do not need to use them often, but you do need to use them. You need to use your authority to draw, and sometimes re-draw, the line in the sand because if you are normally gregarious, the line invariably becomes *less clear* over time.

During one military assignment, we began preparations for a pending Operational Readiness Inspection (ORI). These inspections occurred every two or three years and were important because as the name implies, they evaluated if we *ready to operate* our mission.

As part of our preparation, I instructed my senior staff that I wanted them to do an especially good job with our semi-annual Self Inspection Program. If done properly, through a series of internal reviews (hence, self-inspection), we would know where our problem areas existed and could remediate any weaknesses before the actual inspection began. This particular inspection was in the March timeframe, so the Self Inspection Program for the period ending December 31st would be a timely assessment.

Obviously, we had other things to do on a regular basis besides prepare for our pending inspection. Our normal Accounting and Finance functions could not stop so we had to manage both the preparation phase while actually doing our day-to-day operations. I did remind my staff that the entire 100-person unit relied on their leadership to ensure our two-prong approach was managed effectively.

A key person I relied on was the Quality Assurance Manager for the organization. He worked directly for me and together, we ensured that we built a solid system of internal controls through various means besides the Self Inspection Program. As we neared the December 31st deadline, I asked for an update on where we stood in meeting the suspense. He continued to report moderate progress. I could see where this was going.

On the first workday back after the New Year, I asked the QA Manager for a final status report—again, only partial success. I told him to immediately notify the senior staff to gather in our conference room and not tell them the purpose of the meeting.

I waited in my office, behind closed doors. I did not want to interact with any of them as they normally passed my office for a customary greeting. This was still during the holiday season, most of our Christmas decorations were still up, so it was a festive mood. I could hear the staff greet each other as they made their way toward the conference room for our meeting.

After waiting a few additional minutes to ensure the last straggler was present, I walked into the conference room with the latest status report of the Self Inspection Program. Without any greeting, I used my words in a slow, deliberate fashion. I relayed how I had asked them to complete the self-assessment by the end of the year and they had failed to do so. I expressed my disappointment that they apparently did not take the tasking seriously. Before walking out of the room, I ended my brief message by stating, "If you want to be treated as professionals, you had better start acting like one." The staff sat in stunned silence. I had brought the hammer down hard and unexpectedly.

The ripple effect continued for days. One of the intermediate supervisors had his own meeting with some of the managers to express his displeasure and to chart a course to resolve the matter.

The highest-ranking enlisted person, responsible for a critical part of the overall Self Inspection Program, had also missed the deadline. When it came time to hold our regular weekly staff meeting, I banned him from attending because he still had not finished. That was strong message to the entire staff because he was a key advisor.

The use of my authority in firm tone and actions did not mean that I could not continue using other fingers (influence) as time progressed, and *normalcy* did occur in relatively quick order. Remember, the Talk to the Hand Leadership Concept seeks a balance across the use of leadership influence.

I *had* to draw a line (in this case, a second time) to establish my clear authority as the organizational leader. Missing important deadliness could not be tolerated. The impact of that one incident was more powerful *because* it was a rare occurrence. I used similar situations throughout my career to exert my authority to draw the line when necessary.

In a different assignment (overseas), I called a meeting to discuss an important issue that was coming up in a few months. I wanted us to get ahead of the situation and plan our strategy accordingly. To my surprise, there was sparse attendance by the managers who should have been at the meeting but somehow forgot (most likely) or just blew it off. The timing of this event is important because I had arrived only a few months earlier as the new boss of the organization and I was working hard to emphasize better use of rewards, improving our training program, and lift up lagging morale.

I used this incident to make a point. Yes, I would be there to take care of the people concerns. However, we also had a mission to perform and that was just as important, even more so. I immediately sent word out that I wanted all the appropriate supervisors to meet, but this time in my office. For effect, I let them wait a while before entering the room. I sat down and let them have it. When I called a meeting, they had better be in attendance or have a good excuse not to be present. After I dismissed them, the Superintendent (a Chief Master Sergeant) remained behind. We had a very close relationship and had actually worked together in previous assignments. He felt that I had been perhaps too hard on the group. He reminded me that I had made great strides in turning things around from the previous management. The Chief felt that my tirade could slow or reverse the progress that both of us had made.

I understood where the Chief was coming from and appreciated his willingness to stand up for the troops. At that point, I told him that I had used the missed meeting incident to establish my authority in the new assignment. People needed to know there were *two sides* to my leadership style.

In his book, *The Score Takes Care of Itself: My Philosophy of Leadership*, legendary football Coach Bill Walsh shares his thoughts that further illustrate this point. Coach Walsh noted:

"Having jarred their attention, given them a jolt, I'd get right back to business. Rarely would I get personal or do any damage. It was a somewhat contrived outburst that served like the snarl of a tiger when you get too close to its cage. Used sparingly, it is an effective leadership tool….Ideally, those you lead are driven to excel by the expertise, example, inspiration, and motivation you offer…but sometimes you have to snarl to remind them of the consequences of straying from your standards."[73]

The Significance of Not Giving Away your Authority

As we discussed earlier, authority does not come easily. A leader possesses authority by virtue of their position or corporate rank obtained over time by virtue of their job performance, experience, education, awards, and a continuous record of accomplishment.

During the 1992 Olympics, the United States fielded a Dream Team that included players like Michael Jordan. Coach Mike Krzyzewski, from Duke University, was actually an assistant coach on the team to Chuck Daly who was the head coach. Coach "K" later shared that he was amazed at the respect that Air Jordan himself gave to him and all the coaches. Jordan would say, "Coach, would you please help me with my shot? Thank you, Coach. Thank you very much."[74]

Imagine if Coach "K" instead told Michael Jordan to not talk to him in that manner and just call him "Mike" and took on a "let's just be friends" approach. He would be *giving away his authority* needlessly. As we have already discussed, a leader needs all the power and influence at their disposal just as a person needs all the fingers on their hands. With diminished authority, a leader is less capable to use other elements that go along with it such as issuing discipline or rewards.

When I was a young First Lieutenant, I assumed leadership of a 100-person office including many junior enlisted personnel.

During the first month of my assignment, I noticed that several of the young airmen were getting ready to move a desk from one office to another. They appeared to be waiting on a fourth person so I jumped in and said, "Let's go, I can help you." The Superintendent, a Chief Master Sergeant, who had been directing the detail, urged me to not participate and that the other airman was on his way to assist in the detail.

In my office later, the Chief Master Sergeant went on to elaborate why he was so concerned about my involvement. You see, I had been an enlisted person for eight years before receiving my commission. Therefore, I was a "mustang officer," a term used to describe someone who had been an enlisted person and *then* became an officer. The reference had its root to the half-wild horses of the American plains, especially those of Mexico and California, and came from the Spanish term "Mestengo," –a stray livestock animal.

In hindsight, the Chief was using this incident as a teaching moment, essentially saying, "You're no longer an enlisted man, you're an officer – act like one." Actually, I had left the enlisted ranks nearly five years earlier but I realized the Chief was only looking out for me and grooming a junior officer still learning the ropes. From his perspective, if I started doing details on a regular basis, that would be *giving away my authority* as the new Finance Officer in charge of the entire branch. Fair enough.

Many years later, I faced a situation where I decided it was okay to partake in a detail alongside the enlisted corps. This time, however, I was a new squadron commander and had the rank of Lieutenant Colonel. The installation had recently weathered a tropical storm and each squadron was assigned a geographical area to pick up the mess that the storm had caused. I decided to join the detail that was comprised of *all* enlisted personnel in this case, not just the junior enlisted personnel but non-commissioned officers as well.

I grabbed a rake and some garbage bags and joined my men and women to get the job done. It was also a chance to spend some time with them since I had just arrived as their commander. Later on, the senior enlisted man came into my office to inform me that my act to join "the troops" was perceived as a very positive gesture.

Like most actions, balance is the key. In the case of the latter experience, picking up after a tropical storm, it was an unusual and infrequent event. I used it to demonstrate the importance of teamwork to get the job done. I was not going to assign my name to the detail roster and perform these duties on a regular basis. From these types of experiences, however, I developed some guidelines to help me when it came to the use of authority.

My Own Rule when it comes to Authority

As mentioned, I retired from the United States Air Force after 28 years service that included eight years as a proud enlisted man. Earning my commission was no easy chore as I worked a part-time job, served as a non-commissioned officer, and had a family that required my attention. At night, I took as many as three classes per semester towards a bachelor's degree that enabled me to eventually become an Air Force officer.

Even though I was proud of my achievement, I did not feel I deserved any special treatment because of it. At the same time, I was not going to tolerate when I thought someone was not giving the proper respect to my hard-earned authority. I developed a rule that helped guide me in this respect for years to come.

Authority Rule:
I do not want any *special* treatment or respect given to me for any accomplishments achieved, but I also do not deserve any *less* either.

What should we Call You?

Shortly after military retirement, I took a position as Chief Financial Officer for a national nonprofit agency that supported military personnel and their families. The organizational culture was such that the three executives of the nonprofit (CEO, COO, CFO) were usually retired military officers and were called by their rank (i.e., Colonel Garcia). Calling a retiree by their active duty rank is not uncommon, especially around a military environment.

A few days into the job, I held my first staff meeting with my own team of managers. I set out my expectations and covered other business at the meeting, and at the end, I asked my staff if they had any questions of me. One of them, when it came to his turn, asked me "how should you be addressed?" Imagine if I had just said, "Call me by my first name, of course." The culture and environment in the organization had established a precedence of using military ranks for the retired officers. If the CEO and COO were called by their ranks and I was called by something else, I would be *giving away my authority* unnecessarily.

It was not a matter of an inflated ego, but sticking to the protocol. How would my decision had gone over with the other two, especially my CEO boss (a retired General)? All of a sudden, the new person has put them in an uncomfortable position with their own staffs, "If the CFO can be called by his first name, why aren't we calling you by the same?" There was no issue because I merely replied to the person who raised the question that I preferred to be called by my retired military rank and last name.

Is use of First Name for the Boss okay?

After reading the previous section, you may wonder if you are giving away your authority if you choose to be called by your first name if you are the boss. The situations I described involved a culture (military) that shies away from using first names for higher-ranking non-commissioned officers and officers. I would be going against the grain and giving away my authority if I chose to be called by my first name when everyone else did the opposite.

When I left the military associated nonprofit to work in New Orleans and support the Hurricane Katrina recovery effort, I faced a different culture at FEMA. It did not mean it was wrong, just different. Mr. Jamieson, the Associate FEMA Administrator for Gulf Coast Recovery operations, and head of thousands of workers across four states, was comfortable being called "Gil." Did that make him any less effective as a leader or diminish his authority? Absolutely not. Gil yielded his authority better than most leaders I have ever seen in my career.

Think of it this way. If you fell into the 600-pound silverback gorilla's pit at the zoo, I do not think it would matter if you referred to the gorilla as Mr. Silverback or "G." If he wanted to, he could do me much harm any time he felt like it, no matter *what* you called him.

Final Thoughts on Using Status and Authority

During one overseas assignment, the commanding General of the installation stopped his car at a unit to use the phone. He was in uniform when he walked up to the young troop at the customer service counter and asked to use a phone. The person informed the General that it was squadron policy that customers could not use the phone, just the staff.

The General immediately proceeded to the squadron

120

commander's office. Once there, he told the surprised Major that as commanding General of the installation, that it was *his* base, including all components: its mission, people, money, materials, including phones! Word got out throughout the base of the incident. The 600-pound silverback gorilla had just pounded his chest and roared! Tread lightly and do not take a leader's authority for granted.

The same General described above was a great leader because in addition to using his status and authority wisely, he used other elements of power and influence at his disposal effectively. In the General's case, he "talked to the hand" quite well.

Jeff, the young man mentioned in the Rewards chapter who received a fighter jet incentive ride, had won a prestigious award we had leveraged for the trip. The Chief Master Sergeant of the unit and I were then able to write a nomination for Jeff to receive a Commendation medal at the end of his tour. Normally, there was a progression of sorts in earning awards. The higher ranking an individual, the higher the medal achieved. General Officers normally defer to the unit commander to present medals to their own people.

Nevertheless, I went out on a limb and extended an invitation for the General to attend Jeff's medal ceremony in our unit. To our surprise, the General accepted. The morning of the medal ceremony, I waited in front of our building for the General and his entourage to arrive. When he did, I saluted him smartly and briefly described the schedule of events. Jeff was waiting inside along with a Captain who would call the entire unit to attention when the General entered and then he would read the medal citation. At that time, the General would pin the medal on Jeff.

Instead, the General took both the medal and the citation package from my hands, and proceeded to walk through the glass doors into our large lobby area. I will never forget the scene as I walked behind the General into the building. There is a special atmosphere when the area is called to attention for your installation's commanding officer.

The General, instead of just being a passive bystander, was now fully engaged in the ceremony. He told the unit how proud he was of *their* performance and then focused on Jeff. After a few words of praise, he took the very unusual step of reading the medal citation himself. Afterwards, he walked over to Jeff and pinned the Commendation medal on Jeff's chest.

In this case, this superior officer was superior not because of his rank or position. He was superior because he was using his authority for the benefit of others. He was emphasizing the importance of rewards to motivate others. The General was using several fingers on his hands at once, effectively demonstrating the Talk to the Hand Leadership Concept.

Chapter Seven

Pinky Finger: Forging Relationships

"Technology has given us the ability to reach out over great distances and control actions and people in ways that leaders even fifty years ago could never imagine. But today we have a saying: high tech, low touch. The more technology mediates our communications and contacts, the less personal our relationships."[75]

General Tony Zinni, from his book *Leading the Charge*

General Colin Powell, a great military leader and a true patriot once said: "Management is easy. Leadership is motivating people, turning people on, getting 110% out of a personal relationship."[76]

When someone refers to being wrapped around your finger

(normally the pinky), the impression is usually of a close personal relationship. If two people intertwine their two pinky fingers, it is commonly referred to as a "pinky shake." Younger people often use their pinky fingers to go along with a "pinky swear," implying to keep a solemn promise between two friends.

Fittingly, the pinky *anchors* our Talk to the Hand Leadership Concept. We started with two positive influence factors, the thumb (using rewards), and the index finger (sharing knowledge). The next two fingers, – middle and ring finger – represented *tougher* forms of influence using punishment and authority.

The pinky finger, therefore, nicely rounds out the forms of influence a leader possesses, since the pinky finger represents a leader forging a relationship with those around him or her.

In her book, *Playbook for Success*, former basketball player and Coach Nancy Lieberman offers sound advice to forge a relationship with others. The Hall-of-Famer and motivational speaker and author noted the following:

"You have to have social skills. If you're working in an office and you ride up in the elevator with someone, ask how he or she is. Try to remember people's names. Even if you don't really care, fake it. I know the impression it leaves on me when someone remembers to ask about TJ or my mom. Simple acts of kindness like these are important to building strength and cohesion on your team."[77]

There are numerous ways to forge a good relationship with people. We will highlight a few areas that I have seen work well, based on my own experience, and observations of others. They include:

- Communicate often
- Use your Emotional Intelligence (EQ)
- Have fun at work
- Build Team Pride

Communicate Often

"Communicate, communicate, and then communicate some more."[78]

Bob Nelson, PhD, leadership author

To establish a personal relationship with others, you must communicate with them on a regular basis. For many of my military assignments, I led large groups of people, up to 150 in one overseas assignment. Almost daily, I would start the day off by walking around the office to at least greet the staff and make a quick personal connection. A leader has to be seen (and heard) often.

Admittedly, some of these conversations were brief because if you do the math, if I averaged even five minutes with every employee each day, that alone would take my entire day (100 employees X 5 minutes = 500 minutes or 8.3 hours to be exact).

Therefore, I tried to spread out *longer* conversations with various people throughout the week.

What you communicate is also important. I agree that probing about their outside interests (family, educational pursuits, etc) is important and should occur on a regular basis. However, another purpose of the regular walk-around is to *take your office to them.*

We often talk about *an open door policy*, but how many times does someone jump his or her chain of command and seek out the boss on a matter? Probably, in all likelihood, very infrequently. When you walk around your organization, you *enable* that type of communication to occur. Many times, by being present, the troops would stop and ask me to *share my knowledge* (previously discussed in the index finger chapter) on a subject. Perhaps it was merely to squelch a false rumor that was beginning to spread. Maybe it was to seek my advice on an issue. It did not matter, by being there, I was in a position to communicate with an individual or a group of individuals on a variety of topics, including work or non-work related topics.

"I am glad you do not just talk about babies."

I recall what one individual, Sergeant "Deb," once said that has stuck with me all these years. During our conversations, we would often discuss ways to improve her work area and I tried to encourage her approach for continuous improvement. Then, one morning out of the blue, the female Staff Sergeant abruptly told me, "I am glad you do not just talk about babies." When she said this I was a bit perplexed, and it must have shown on my face, because she elaborated on her comment.

She indicated that the previous officer, a female Captain, would also take the time to walk around the office and communicate with the workforce. The Sergeant was disappointed however, when the Captain got around to *her* desk, she would often *only* talk about family and children. In the Captain's mind, she was communicating on a personal level (making a pinky connection) woman-to-woman.

To the Sergeant, however, it was patronizing because she noticed that the Captain would tend to talk work-related matters to the male employees. It also meant that the Captain did not receive the good ideas that the Sergeant had to improve the office or a quick update on how things were going in her area. As a result, the Captain might overlook the Sergeant for a challenging assignment since the Captain only talked only to her about "babies." Like most things, a healthy balance is the key when communicating with males and females on both personal and professional matters.

The importance of Emotional Intelligence (EQ)

As we stated earlier, acquiring and sharing knowledge through education and professional certification is important, but your ability to assess people's feelings is also important to a leader.

Daniel Goleman is a pioneer in the Emotional Intelligence (EQ) research and teachings. He and his colleagues attempted to examine the relationship between EQ and leadership performance in the workplace. Objective criteria was developed that included profitability of the organizations they led. The results were striking.[79]

Here is what Goleman had to say in describing the importance of Emotional Intelligence (EQ):

"...the most effective leaders are alike in one way: they all have a high degree of what has come to be known as *emotional intelligence*. Without it, a person can have the best training in the world, an incisive, analytical mind, and an endless supply of smart ideas, but he still won't make a great leader."[80]

Daniel Goleman, author of the best-seller, *Emotional Intelligence*

~~~~~~~~~~~

Our smallest finger can do the most good.

When Goleman calculated the ingredients of excellent performance - (1) technical skills, (2) IQ, and (3) EQ, it was EQ that proved twice as important as the other two. As Goleman explains, "It was once thought that the components of emotional intelligence were 'nice to have' in business leaders. But now we know that, for the sake of performance, these are ingredients that leaders 'need to have'."[81]

The five components of emotional intelligence and some of the hallmarks for each component include:[82]

- Self-Awareness (self-confidence but self-deprecating sense of humor)
- Self-Regulation (trustworthiness and integrity)
- Motivation (optimism, strong desire to achieve)
- Empathy (cross-cultural sensitivity)
- Social Skill (expert in building teams and leading change)

Whereas IQ can help you to read a book, EQ can help when you are trying to read (and lead) people. Both are important, but possessing and using EQ can take a leader a long way.

EQ Makes a Difference for an Air Force Academy Cadet

As I mentioned in the Knowledge chapter, I tried to stay ahead of the cadets in the Leadership course I taught at the Air Force Academy. By doing outside reading and research on my own time, I could add supplemental readings to the course materials and keep it fresh in the classroom.

During this time, a national magazine published a landmark article on Emotional Intelligence (EQ). I made copies of the relatively short article and handed them out to each of the cadets in my class. As part of their overall course grade, the students were required to complete ten journal entries throughout the semester. They could use a journal entry to describe a leadership situation that they observed at the Academy. Alternatively, sometimes I would assign a topic for them to write on for their journal. On this occasion, I assigned the cadets to write their thoughts on the new concept of EQ that was not part of our textbook or curriculum.

> Whereas IQ can help you to read a book, EQ can help when you are trying to read (and lead) people. Both are important, but possessing and using EQ can take a leader a long way.

Most of the cadets were seniors in my classroom, and for some reason, I had my share of football players as part of the student roster. I am still amazed at how these NCAA Division I level college athletes could balance athletic participation with military training, an intense academic load, and other activities that made up cadet life.

One player's journal entry on the EQ assignment made a huge impact on him and on me as well. He was one of those students who did not speak much in class, but at the same time, was always polite and good-natured. His test scores and written papers were consistently "average."

As a senior, he was set to graduate in a few months and enter active duty as a newly minted Second Lieutenant. Up to now, the only real benchmark for his capabilities revolved around his grade point average and class ranking. The cadets even received similar reporting on their military training. Based on those standards, he felt inadequate and unprepared for active duty life.

After reading the article on EQ, however, the cadet wrote in his journal that his perspective about himself had changed dramatically. His words practically jumped from the page as I read them. Later when I talked to him about his journal entry, he voiced the same enthusiasm. "Captain, I got this EQ stuff down cold," he professed. "People are always coming around to my room and I am really good at listening to them and helping to solve their problems. I get along with everybody and I seek to understand how they are feeling." It warmed my heart that a simple outside article, for a journal assignment no less, made such a positive impact on a future officer. The EQ concept gave him renewed confidence that he could succeed on active duty. IQ, in the form of grades and book smarts is no doubt important. Perhaps even *more* important, is the ability to connect with others.

In our Talk to the Hand Leadership Concept, we emphasize use of *all the influence factors* (fingers). In the Knowledge chapter, we emphasized that a leader should strive to acquire knowledge through formal education, professional certifications, and the like, that is represented by the index finger. The same holds true for the pinky finger representing forging a personal relationship with those around us and those we lead. As Goleman himself concluded:

"It is fortunate, then, that emotional intelligence can be learned. The process is not easy. It takes time and, most of all, commitment. But the benefits that come from having a well-developed emotional intelligence, both for the individual and for the organization, make it worth the effort."[83]

Other Factors that Influence Pinky Power: Humor and Team Pride

I have to admit, I cannot think of a day at work that I did not laugh at least once. Laughing reduces stress, gets our blood flowing, and combats fatigue and boredom. I even found a way to use it in the classroom at the Air Force Academy.

As an Adjunct Instructor for the Department of Behavioral Sciences, I had a primary job *outside* of the Dean of the Faculty organization. I participated in faculty staff meetings, training, etc, but for most of my day, I had other duties and responsibilities. Our administrative assistant ("Cindy") in my primary office often asked about the class I taught so I arranged for her to join me the next morning. By coincidence, that day would be April 1st, or April Fool's Day.

We plotted our strategy. Cindy would pose as a classroom evaluator for the Dean of the Faculty. She found an old briefcase in the storage closet that looked like something used in the 1960s. It was plain, bulky, and a bit torn. In other words, it was ideal for our prank. It was large enough to hold a dozen donuts and a container of orange juice that I occasionally snuck into the classroom as a treat.

The next morning, we met in our office before walking over across the terrazzo to the classroom. Cindy dressed for the scheme perfectly, wearing very conservative clothing, glasses, and little make-up. As we entered the classroom, Cindy carrying the briefcase, found a seat in the back of the classroom. "Class, we have a visitor today," I announced. "Miss Cindy Jones is an evaluator for the Dean, who personally asked her to provide an assessment on randomly selected instructors. So just be yourselves and pretend she is not here." Cindy reached into the briefcase and brought out a notepad and a pen to begin taking notes for her "evaluation."

On occasion, I would begin the class with one of David Letterman's "Top 10 Lists." I made a transparent slide and showed it on the projector screen. They were corny but the cadets always got a kick out of them and burst out laughing. For this day, I chose the best material: *A Top 10 list of how college athletes cheat in the classroom.* I covered up the full list and then read one of them at a time, pausing for effect after each one. The cadets had no idea what to do. Since I told them to be themselves, should they laugh at the silly jokes? On the other hand, because the evaluator was in the room, should they *not* laugh because she might perceive it as improper classroom protocol? The cadets played it safe and chose the latter – to sit quietly.

Cindy, meanwhile, was acting up a storm. She would shake her head, mumble something, and then write down notes furiously on her pad. The cadets kept looking at me, the projector screen, and then over to the "evaluator." Cindy later told me that she could barely contain from not laughing herself.

Finally, after one of her snide comments beneath her breath, I asked her if anything was wrong. Cindy informed me that this was not what she expected and that the Dean (a General Officer) would not be very pleased when she reported to him. I told her that this was still *my* classroom and I would instruct the way I wanted to. If she did not like it, she was welcome to just leave (we were improvising at that point). She picked up her notepad and stormed out of the classroom, leaving the large briefcase behind. "We will see about this," her parting remarks out the door.

The cadets' eyes were as big as saucers. One cadet asked, "Sir, are you going to be in trouble?" I continued fussing about the need for an evaluator in the first place and headed towards the briefcase left behind. I opened it and after a minute of looking through the case, brought out the donuts and orange juice.

When the cadets let out an audible sigh of relief, Cindy

stepped back in the classroom after waiting quietly outside, and gave a hearty "April Fool's!" She stayed and helped to pass out the refreshments as we continued with our classroom discussion.

More Use of Humor

On another occasion at the Academy, I coordinated an idea with the Lieutenant assigned to work with me. Lieutenant "Kevin" was a very sharp young officer and I enjoyed working with him for about four months before he headed off to pilot training school. He would eventually earn a fighter pilot position, a career he wanted to pursue in the Air Force for a long time. A recent Academy graduate himself, he was very helpful to me in my primary role as a Regional Director of Admissions.

The morning of my Leadership class, I handed a video tape to Lieutenant "Kevin" and instructed him show it at the beginning of class. The tape contained a five-minute cartoon that I had recorded over the weekend. It was one of those clips that you could not help but laughing at. It was slapstick kind of humor with the characters' eyes popping out, or their jaw dropping to the ground, in response to the events around them. Silly but funny.

I advised Lieutenant "Kevin" to walk into the classroom, take attendance, and then tell them that I was issuing a challenge to them. The challenge was to determine the *significance* of the cartoon that they were about to see. If they got it right, I would consider eliminating one of the ten mandatory journal entries that was required for the class. The "L.T." got the cartoon clip going and stepped back to watch the group interact.

As expected, the students were laughing at the animation, while at the same time trying to analyze the cartoon itself. They were searching for any meaning of the *characters or story line* (they were not going to get far there!). They had boxed themselves in with their line of thinking.

When I arrived, I asked them for a group consensus on what they felt was the significance of the cartoon. After hearing their ideas, I gave them the answer that I was really seeking. The cartoon itself was insignificant; it was the *purpose* behind showing it. I shared with the Leadership class that soon they would be entering active duty as Second Lieutenants and leaders of men and women. Their cadet training, and understandably so, tended to emphasize order and discipline. The population they managed was within the constraints of the Academy itself. Soon, they would be leading a more diverse group of people. The purpose of showing a 5-minute cartoon to the class was to break up the monotony, do something a bit different, and stimulate their thinking ability. Actor John Cleese said it very well when he noted:

"I think the main evolutionary significance of our sense of humor is that it gets us from the closed mode to the open mode quicker than anything else. I think we all know laughter brings relaxation and humor makes us playful."[84]

The formal lesson that day was actually a good one, on the importance of values. I hope there was another lesson for the cadets – that it was okay to have a sense of humor and a little fun as a means to connect with people and get creative juices flowing.

Watch out for the Sandman

"Here's what the overly serious people miss: the fun, the creativity, the lighthearted ideas, the intuition, the good spirits, the easy energy, and the quick laughter that brings people close to each other."[85]

Steve Chandler, from the book *100 Ways to Motivate Others*

Years ago, there was a popular television series called "Showtime at the Apollo." It was one of the earliest versions of shows like "The Gong Show," and then later the "American Idol." Amateur acts performed live at the historic Apollo Theater in Harlem, New York. As part of the show, a person called "the Sandman," would dance his way on stage to his music and bring out a cane to pull out the hapless performers as they were booed off stage.

In a recent engagement for a client, I used the Sandman story to keep things light but at the same time drive home a point to my team. If we had an important update or formal presentation to the client, I playfully warned that we needed to keep the Sandman away – no *cane* for us.

I remember one time where we were set to give such a

briefing but it kept being rescheduled due to the client's schedule. Each time, we were adequately prepared and ready to go from our end. As fate would have it, when the meeting was finally scheduled, everything went wrong. We were in a room that was not big enough (people were crowded in together), it was stuffy and hot in the room, and to make matters worse, the computer in the room went on the blink. As a result, we had to improvise and use hard copy handouts.

As we walked back to our office space, a bit dejected on the presentation, I teased the group that we had been able to keep the Sandman away for so long, that he acted out his vengeance when he did show up. In reality, we had no control over the room dynamics, and the team did the best it could under the circumstances. Using the Sandman analogy kept things light and our spirits up. Rather than sulking about a bad break, we were able to laugh about it and move on to fight another day. Humor can definitely bring people closer together if used properly.

"Successful leaders take their work and responsibilities very seriously indeed. You don't get to the top of a company, and then take that company to the top of its industry, without taking care of business. At the same time, successful leaders view fun in the workplace as essential to innovation, risk-taking, team spirit, and performance. When people have fun together, they are more likely to accomplish extraordinary things together."[86]

Oren Harari, *The Powell Principles: 24 Lessons from Colin Powell*

Team Pride: The Lightning Bolt

In their book, *The Great Workplace*, authors Michael Burchell and Jennifer Robin describe in great places to work, people are proud of their company's products, mission, service, or people. The benefit of such pride spills back to the organization itself. For one thing, employees in such companies are less willing to leave and high turnover is a direct cost to the business. Employees even described that they would like to retire from the firm.[87]

Sometimes you can combine a bit of humor and build pride at the same time. During one recent assignment, I told the team that we should not just produce a timely and quality product, it should be *the best*. To emphasize the point, I reminded them of what sprinter Husain Bolt (from Jamaica) had accomplished at the 2008 Summer Olympics.

Bolt not only won three gold medals in the 100 and 200-meter sprints, and as part of the 400 meter relay team, but he set world records in each of the events. His margin of victory in some of the races was especially spectacular. Nicknamed the Lightning Bolt, he began a trademark pose after his victories that caricaturized a bolt of lightning.

I encouraged the team to reach *that* level of standard. Not good, not very good, not even great, -- reach to be *the best*. Soon, when we hit our mark, somebody would invariably point to the sky to imitate Husain Bolt's trademark move. It was our way of bonding by using a special communication means that encouraged each other towards peak performance. It was also a powerful means to keep us focused to achieve our very best, and the results reflected our approach.

Using the Pinky (forging relationship) is Valuable to Both Parties

"We will work harder and more effectively for people we like. And we like them in direction proportion to how they make us feel."[88]

From the book, *A Leader's Legacy*

Some of you may be convinced that an "old school" philosophy where a leader *does not need* to establish a relationship with their followers is the best approach. In this thought process, a leader's authority is sufficient to propel others toward the desired outcome. My own personal experience and in evolving leadership research tells a different story.

One of my early military tours was to Osan Air Base in South Korea. It was a demanding assignment for many reasons. Being a remote tour, most people were separated from their families for one full year. The constant turnover in staff throughout the year also made it hard to build continuity in purpose and processes.

Despite these challenges, we also recognized the importance of our mission. We considered ourselves at the "tip of the spear." If the North Koreans decided to invade across the 38th parallel (demilitarized zone), our job was to slow them down enough until the reinforcements from other parts of the globe could engage. As a result, we were tight as a group and in many ways like family. One visiting inspector from our headquarters in Hawaii told me that he was surprised that our morale was higher than all the other bases, including those in Japan or Hawaii itself!

One of the military personnel assigned to the front office with me was a Sergeant we called "Big Lou." We had a great relationship built on mutual respect and showing true concern for each other, as was the case for the other troops. A few months after I arrived in country, the Captain who was the Finance Officer, rotated back to the states. In the interim period before L.C. Williams (mentioned earlier) arrived to replace the Captain, I was the acting Finance Officer.

It was a tradition in the office, that on payday, the Finance Officer would inspect the troops in the lobby for uniform compliance, haircuts, shoeshine, etc. On the first payday that I would inspect the enlisted corps, of all days, I overslept. I never oversleep but I faced my own "Sandman" that morning. It was only a few minutes past the start of the workday, but I knew that I would be late for the inspection by around 15 minutes if I hurried.

I rushed down the hall to the only phone on the floor and called the office. Fortunately, "Big Lou" must have heard the phone ring in the front office from the lobby because he answered it after a few rings. I told him honestly that I had overslept and would be there as soon as I could.

Consider what "Big Lou" could have done to me at that

point. It would have been very easy for him to walk back to the assembled troops and announce to the group to "take five" because the new Finance Officer had overslept. Any comments like that would have damaged my credibility and trustworthiness with the entire office.

When I finally made it into the office from the short distance from my barracks, I went straight into our administrative section to get my bearings on what to do next. Sensing my arrival, "Big Lou" calmly approached me and escorted me to my office, away from the others so they could not hear our conversation. He immediately calmed me down and told me not to worry.

The Sergeant told me that after my phone call, he went back into the lobby area and informed the troops that I had been called into a meeting at the office of the Special Investigations Agent (occasionally did occur). The meeting should just take a few minutes so the group should just hang tight. Yes, it was a "white lie" on his part but the gesture meant a lot to me for doing his best to *have my back*. Obviously, I never forgot it. I got through the inspection without any problems and the day went on as normal.

This is what forging a *personal* relationship is about. James Kouzes and Barry Posner describe it this way in their book, *A Leader's Legacy*:"

"When we talk to people about the leaders they admire – the ones they'd stay up late for, the ones they'd bust their butts for, the ones they'd die for – we never, ever hear anyone tell us, 'Well I hated that woman, but I'd follow her to the ends of the earth.' Or, 'He was a real jerk, but I sure was inspired to do my best for him.' The leaders people *want* to follow are the ones for whom they have genuine affection'. "[89]

During the same Korean assignment, I faced an awkward situation shortly after my arrival. As a young Lieutenant, I was assigned as the Deputy Finance Officer supporting the Finance Officer (normally a Captain). As mentioned previously, being a one-year remote assignment, there was constant turnover of personnel, including the Captain's position. Before I arrived, the outgoing Captain arranged that during the interim period before Captain L.C. Williams arrived, that the interim role would pass to the Chief Master Sergeant in the unit. The Chief clearly had the vast experience and knowledge required to assume the duties. What complicated matters was my own background to consider.

The unit paperwork showed an inbound Second Lieutenant to serve as the Deputy. In many cases, the Lieutenant is a freshly minted officer out of the Academy or an ROTC unit with practically no active duty experience. In my case, however, I had eight years prior enlisted time in the Finance career field, and another two years as a Deputy at a stateside unit. I had also pinned on the rank of First Lieutenant a few weeks after my arrival. With 10 years of experience, a recently acquired Masters in Business Administration, and my recent promotion, the outgoing Captain determined that I was better suited to lead the office during the interim three-month period.

Admittedly, many people, including the Chief were taken

back by the sudden change and felt it was a slight to the high-ranking enlisted person. I certainly understood their feelings and did my best to minimize the impact. I reached out to the Chief and embraced him as a valuable partner in running the office. We worked together as a team and I regularly used his experience and advice.

In those days, an Air Force Finance Officer literally held an account with the U. S. Treasury. The select few, about a hundred in the entire Air Force, received a personalized signature dye. These special cast plates engraved their signature on thousands of green government checks issued each month since there were too many to sign. This was before the use of electronic funds transfer that sent disbursements directly to the payee's bank account.

There was a custom to issue a government check to a new Finance Officer, with the significance being that *his or her* signature was on the check. By giving a dollar-bill to the cashier, the Disbursing staff could turn around and issue the hard copy green check without any impropriety. Very few enlisted personnel became a Finance Officer.

One day I called the staff together for a surprise meeting. I had arranged with the Disbursing staff to issue a one-dollar check made out to the Chief, and used *his* signature dye on the negotiable instrument itself. I then had the check framed.

When I called him up from the gathered crowd, the Chief seemed taken aback. I indicated that it was quite an honor for his selection as the acting Finance Officer, a rare tribute to any enlisted man. He had clearly earned that tribute based on a long and distinguished career. I wanted all the office to know that he still deserved special recognition, regardless of a change in the assignment of the Finance Officer position to someone else.

When I handed him the framed check with his signature on it, he seemed genuinely humbled and appreciative of the gesture. In my mind, he deserved his special moment. Weeks later, the Chief had arranged for a nice office social function at the senior enlisted private club on base. During the evening, when we had a few moments to ourselves, the Chief shared that he truly enjoyed working with me and he appreciated my honesty.

By using my own emotional intelligence (EQ), I expressed empathy for the situation involving the Chief. No one suggested I hold the event to present him the "ceremonial one-dollar check," but it seemed the right thing to do. It meant a lot to me that we had established a mutually respectful working and personal relationship from a less than ideal beginning.

Final Thoughts on Forging Relationships (Pinky Power)

"When we act effectively as leaders, those around us bond with us – not because of our position or title in the organization, but because of their relationship with us. But that kind of emotional connection can only occur when you are genuinely concerned about others...Being nice to others is fundamental."[90]

From *You Don't Need a Title to be a Leader*, by Mark Sanborn

In order to forge relationships with others, leaders can use methods we described in this chapter, such as frequent and sincere communication, EQ factors such as empathy for others and social skill, and letting their guard down to have fun at work while still instilling team pride. In some circles, this approach is referred to as *soft management* versus tough-guy tactics. In his Harvard Business Review article, "The Hard Work of Being a Soft Manager," William Peace shares the following, "I believe that openness is a productive management technique and that intentional vulnerability is an effective management style. The soft management I believe in and do my best to practice is a matter of making hard choices and of accepting personal responsibility for decisions."[91]

In her book, *Women on Top: How Women Entrepreneurs are Rewriting the Rules of Business Success*, Margaret Heffernan, addresses the issue of women being perceived as *too soft* to make it in the business world.

"Many claim that our 'female' qualities hold us back inside large traditional corporations....I would argue that, far from being a problem, such behavior represent a solution because when we run our own businesses, where ownership already bestows power and where we can more easily determine the values of our companies, these same characteristics turn out to be tremendously advantageous. We are not dominant, which means that we aren't threatened when our employees know more than we do. We are collaborative and understand that part of being collaborative is knowing when to bite our lips. By not singing our own praises, we leave space for more than one hero in every company. By not hogging the spotlight, we let whole teams shine."[92]

Forging a personal relationship does take an effort on your part. I have always believed it is actually *easier* to be a "tough" boss than one seeking to really connect with his or her people. What is so hard about staying in a bad mood, acting grumpy, being negative, and saying "no" to everybody and everything? Anybody can do that!

On the other hand, leaders who try to figure out ways to establish and build a relationship with their people probably *do* work harder. I also believe, however, that others will want to work much *harder for them*.

The examples cited during this chapter were meant to stimulate your own thought process on the various pinky influence factor. The *exact* measures you take are not that important. What *is* important is develop a relationship worthy of a pinky shake.

In the Talk to the Hand Leadership Concept, you are encouraged to use all our available power and influence factors in the same manner you routinely use *all your fingers* to make things happen with your hands. Using one finger does not prevent you from using another one later on.

~~~~~~~~~~
Leaders who try to figure out ways to establish and build a relationship with their people probably *do* work harder. I also believe, however, that others will want to work much *harder for them*.

Chapter Eight

Elvis-Like Hand Gesture: a Leadership Tip

Elvis on Stage

In the summer of 1976, while stationed at a base in Tucson, Arizona, I had an opportunity to see Elvis Presley in concert – about a year before the "King" passed away. He put on quite a show that afternoon even though he had slowed down just a bit. A black belt in Karate, he would often make sweeping kicks and hand gestures on stage. He, like many celebrities, would use the hand symbol to express "I love you." We are now going to create an Elvis-like hand gesture to enhance our Talk to The Hand Leadership Concept. With your *palm facing towards you*, fully extend out your five fingers. In a counterclockwise motion, rotate your hand to the left ninety degrees so that the thumb is facing straight up. Finally, tuck in the middle finger and the ring finger. If you have ever saw Elvis perform live, or viewed him on television, our gesture resembles the kind of move that Elvis did on stage, often on bended knee for emphasis.

We are going to use that Elvis-like gesture to form a tip when it comes to seeking the right combination of fingers to use with the Talk to the Hand Leadership Concept. At this point, let us recap what we discussed and analyzed in the previous chapters. Using both personal experiences and outside research, we built a leadership framework. The Talk to the Hand Leadership Concept suggests a person can be a more effective leader through a balanced use of available power factors, represented by the five fingers described below.

Thumb: As in "Thumbs up," – **Rewards**
Index finger: "Thinking" gesture – **Sharing Knowledge**
Middle finger: "Negative" gesture – **Using Punishment**
Ring finger: "Wedding ring" represents **Status and Authority**
Pinky: "Pinky shake" – **Forging Relationships**

We are now ready to separate the five power factors, represented by each finger, into two groups: (1) Proactive/more positive, and (2) Reactive/more negative.

Don't be Cruel

In their excellent book, *The Great Workplace: How to Build it, How to Keep it, and Why it Matters*, authors Michael Burchell and Jennifer Robin, search for what makes organizations special. In one example, Rob Burton (Hoar Construction) shared the following: "When it comes to specific issues, I think one of the biggest mistakes that CEOs make is to look forward to the power and authority that they're given. My advice is, sure that's true, but take that and put it in your pocket because you don't need to use it. When you need to use it, it's there and everybody knows that. You can say no when you want to. The better thing to do is to forget about it and stay humble and go to work with your friends and get the job done. That's been my philosophy about it. It's not an ego trip. It's a lifestyle."[93]

Our Elvis-type gesture has three fingers *pointing out*, and two fingers *tucked in*. The chart below (figure 5) shows each of the fingers that make up the Talk to the Hand Leadership Concept.

Positive Factors		Less Positive Factors	
Finger	**Influence Factor**	**Finger**	**Influence Factor**
Thumb	Using Rewards	*Middle*	Using Punishment
Index	Sharing Knowledge	*Ring*	Using Authority
Pinky	Building Relationships		
Proactive Approach		**Reactive Approach**	

Figure 5

By grouping the fingers into one of two categories (positive or less positive), suggests which influence factors should be used more proactively and which ones a leader should be more reactive in their use. The tool that will enable us to do so borrows from a hand gesture of the type used by Elvis (shown at figure 6).

Positive Factors – Be Proactive (Fingers out)		
Finger	**Types of Power**	**Visual**
Thumb	Using Rewards	
Index	Sharing Knowledge	
Pinky	Building Relationships	
Less Positive Factors – Be More Reactive (Fingers in)		
Finger	**Types of Power**	**Visual**
Middle	Using Punishment	
Ring	Using Authority	
Factors Combined		**Visual**
Elvis-Type Gesture		

Figure 6

When to be Proactive as a Leader

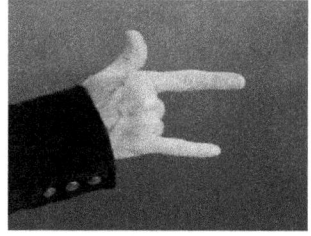

Although all of our five power factors are important, a leader should be more forward leaning in three of them.

- Promoting the use of Rewards (thumb)
- Sharing Knowledge (index finger)
- Forging a Relationship with others (pinky)

The reason a leader should be proactive in these areas is it takes an effort on your part to ensure that they happen. For example, developing and maintaining a robust rewards program requires a commitment of time and resources. If you are not careful, other day-to-day activities tend to overwhelm us and the "good idea" never happens. As mentioned previously, a reward is important because the followers offered something tangible to earn the incentive in the first place. If you do not proactively build a recognition system, your people may reason why should they continue giving their all if you are not reciprocating in turn.

The same holds true for acquiring and sharing our knowledge with others. When I was on active duty, in order to be promoted to Major, the expectation was that you completed your Masters Degree. Many officers put off pursuing the advanced degree until the last possible time period. By then, they often had a spouse, children, and challenging job responsibilities as a senior Captain.

Fortunately, after finishing my Bachelors Degree and entering active duty as a Second Lieutenant, I decided to keep going to school and finished a Masters in Business Administration. A few weeks after the graduation, I shipped off to South Korea. I cannot imagine dealing with the challenges of that tough assignment while trying to complete the Masters program at the same time.

Finally, it takes a positive effort to forge a relationship with other people. Saying "hi" to someone in the hall is not going to cut it. A friend of mine, recently promoted to a senior government position, borrowed a practice I shared with him that works for me. When taking over an organization, I developed a simple introduction form that I asked current employees to fill out for me. The sheet asked the team member numerous questions, including the following,

- How would you like to be called? (Jane, Mrs. Smith, etc)
- Do you have family? (What are *their* names?)
- What works well in this organization?
- What improvements would you like to see?
- What are your intermediate and long-term goals?

During one assignment, on my very first day in the new organization, I went around and shook hands and met with all 150 employees. It took most of my time, but at the end of the day, the

Chief who accompanied me told me that it really set the tone that I valued them on a personal level. A *reactive* approach would have been to rationalize that eventually I would meet each of them over time since it was a three-year assignment.

In summary, a leader should be proactive in the influence factors of rewarding the workforce, acquiring and sharing knowledge, and establishing a strong personal relationship with their people. Being proactive means consciously pursuing these objectives on a daily basis.

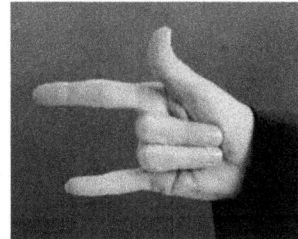

When to be Reactive as a Leader

If it is best to be proactive in the three powers and influence factors represented by the thumb, index finger, and the pinky, then logically we would be more selective in use of the other two;

- Using authority to draw the line (ring finger)

- Punish when that line is crossed (middle finger)

There are times when a leader should use power to push the use of mainly positive factors such as rewards, knowledge, or to forge a relationship. There will be other times, however, when a leader should exert authority or administer punishment.

A leader will face situations that call for stern steps to draw the line in the sand, or to deal with incidents when that line is crossed as shown below.

Use Authority to *draw* the line:

Use Discipline and Punishment *when that line is crossed*:

X: Inappropriate behavior

In his excellent book, *100 Ways to Motivate Others*, author Steve Chandler, calls on a leader to be a "Bad Cop" on occasion. This means having direct conversations to a failing subordinate like, "I believe in you. I know what you can do. When you don't do it, you let yourself and the team down. I won't allow that. Time to wake up."[94]

Chandler goes on to suggest that Bad Cop tactics, in our case use of punishment or exerting our authority, is best used only when you need to do so.

"Obviously, you don't call on Bad Cop every day. Only after every Good Cop approach is exhausted. But Bad Cop can be a great wake-up call to someone who has never been challenged in life to be the best she can be. And once the Bad Cop session is over, and the person is back in the game, giving it a good effort, bring Good Cop back right away to complete the process."[95]

Use the Elvis Leadership Gesture for Effective Balance

"The key to successful leadership today is influence not authority."[96]

Kenneth Blanchard

In the Talk to the Hand Leadership Concept, you bring out the middle finger and ring finger in reaction to an event that you cannot choose to let go. In our Elvis-like gesture, these two middle fingers are tucked in (since not normally used) while the other three are fully exposed ready to be used robustly. The Elvis

Leadership Gesture Tip then is essentially the following mantra:

~~~~~~~~~~~

Be an upbeat leader until the time calls for you to be otherwise.

"Psychologists have studied reward and punishment for a century, and the bottom line is perfectly clear: Reward works better."[97]

Harvard Business Review article

From their book, *A Leader's Legacy*, Kouzes and Posner reinforce the *positive approach* leadership style:

"Our research, and practically everyone else's on the subject, clearly shows that people perform significantly more effectively when their leaders treat them with dignity and respect, listen to them, support them, recognize them, make them feel important, build their skills, and show confidence in them. Likeability is a major factor in being successful in just about every endeavor in life."[98]

At the same time, Kouzes and Posner acknowledge the limits of a positive approach, and describe times when we must react in a negative manner. They conclude;

"When it comes to leading others, it'd be terrific if we only had to do the things that brought great joy to people's lives and to our own. A tough truth about leading – and one that doesn't get talked about enough – is that sometimes you hurt others and sometimes you get hurt. You can't hit the delete key and eliminate these times from your job. You can't delegate them to others. They come with the territory."[99]

The Elvis Leadership Tip mantra, *be an upbeat leader until the time calls for you to be otherwise*, is reinforced by the Elvis-type gesture itself. The two fingers tucked in mean you do not *normally* use them. They are the ring finger representing authority and the middle finger that symbolizes the use of discipline.

By clenching these fingers back, you are consciously putting them away. You do not actively seek to use them and you are better off using the positive factors instead. However, we must understand that when situations come our way that *force our hand*, we must unclench the two middle fingers and use them appropriately. When the matter is resolved, we *pull them back* again.

An Elvis Leadership Lesson from the Commandant of Cadets

As mentioned previously, I taught a Leadership course at the Air Force Academy in Colorado Springs, Colorado for several years. I truly enjoyed the experience and the opportunity to teach at the prestigious military academy ranks as a special highlight in my 28-year career.

I attempted to stretch the cadets beyond their readings and assignments found in the normal curriculum. I challenged them to develop a formal presentation for their ideas to make the Academy a better learning environment. To make the assignment even more meaningful, I would invite the Commandant of Cadets, a General Officer, to the classroom to hear the cadet briefings. Although an extremely busy person, I was pleased that he attended the presentations as often as his schedule permitted.

On one occasion, the General was unable to attend the briefing. I advised the cadets to put their recommendation in writing into a "talking paper" format and I submitted it to the Commandant on their behalf. Shortly thereafter, I was surprised to receive a memorandum from the General who requested that they personally brief him in his conference room.

This particular leadership class had several football players in the group. They felt during the home football games that they could not feel the energy you would expect at a contest held in their own stadium. The group rationalized that if the senior cadets could dress in *civilian clothes*, rather than the full service uniforms, the cadets would be more animated in the stands. In turn, the cadet student body would incite the rest of the crowd to cheer even louder – leading to a true competitive home field advantage. To me, their recommendation seemed reasonable at the time.

Unfortunately, the Commandant did not think it was a good idea. The cadets struggled to remain enthusiastic about their proposal, while remaining respectful to the General Officer. I decided to jump in and tried to lend them some assistance. "Sir, the cadets just want to have some fun," I offered.

The Commandant of Cadets looked firmly at me and retorted, "Did it occur to you, I don't want them to have fun. This is a military academy after all. We are teaching them character and discipline, and that separates us from other universities." I learned a valuable lesson from a respected senior officer that there should be balance in the use of leadership power. I was too quick to "seek fun" (pinky power) whereas the General was looking at the big picture. He was right and exercised his authority as the Commandant of Cadets. My viewpoint as a Captain was different and admittedly shortsighted.

My own Use of the Elvis Leadership Tip

Throughout my tour as a squadron commander, I tried to make the workplace an enjoyable and rewarding place to work. I remember one Halloween where people dressed up, and some of us walked over to the child daycare center to have fun with the kids in our costumes.

During one office Christmas party, I organized a small group to dance at the gathering. We were not very good but the audience seemed to get a kick of out our antics.

During this time-period, our youngest troop in the squadron named "Don" got into some trouble involving alcohol. He was a fine young man and I felt a special fondness for him. Airman "Don" was a solid performer at work, a bit reserved and always polite and courteous. When I got the call that he was involved with the incident that also included fighting, there was no wiggle room to let it go. I could not tolerate his unacceptable behavior so we administered necessary punishment swiftly and appropriately.

Only a few months later, we were about to undergo our Operational Readiness Inspection. We had been preparing for the inspection for about six months. As we neared the last week before the Inspector General (IG) staff arrived from command headquarters, we still needed to make one important decision. Who would deliver the important orientation briefing to the IG staff when they arrived on the first day of the inspection?

The briefing was very important for several reasons. First, it was our opportunity to establish a good first impression on the visitors. A good orientation often set the tone for the rest of the inspection. Conversely, missing your mark could leave a negative impression that would be hard to overcome. Second, the orientation was a means to highlight our achievements of the past several years and again, leave a positive image with the IG staff.

In many cases, the squadron commander gives the

orientation since the inspection team is evaluating his or her unit. Sometimes, the commander may choose to delegate the brief to a company grade officer such as a Captain or First Lieutenant. After thinking about the options, I decided to go a very different route. I would choose the junior enlisted person in the 75-person squadron to give the important IG orientation briefing. That person was "Don," the enlisted man who only a few months ago had been punished for his drinking incident.

When I told him of my decision, he seemed a bit hesitant. Certainly, he had not faced such a daunting challenge before in his short military career. He would be carrying the burden of the entire squadron to receive a high mark in the inspection on his young shoulders. I encouraged "Don" that he would represent our unit with distinction and we would be with him every step of the way.

After finalizing the power point presentation, we provided the young Airman his script so he could begin to practice it. Our squadron had recently purchased a *smart board* that allowed embedded videos into the presentation. He could merely tap a still photo and it would stream with video and even music. It was quite impressive but also another element that "Don" would need to manage during the briefing.

A couple of days before the inspection commenced, I had "Don" practice the briefing in front of his fellow squadron team members. It was not only a chance for him to do a dry run or two, but it allowed the squadron to see and hear what we had put together for the orientation. After all, in my mind, we were *all* being inspected, not just the commander and senior staff. Besides, much of the "bragging" items came directly from their hard work. I was proud that during the dry runs, the squadron provided good suggestions to improve the presentation while at the same time, offering their own words of encouragement to "Don."

Finally, the big day arrived, and the senior team gathered in our conference room to welcome the visiting IG staff to our squadron. I have to admit, there were a few butterflies going through my stomach that morning. Had we done everything possible to adequately prepare for the big inspection? I realized we had done our best. The facility was in good order and the troops were especially sharp looking for our big moment.

As I walked up to the front of the room, I made just a few opening remarks. The inspectors seemed a bit surprised when I then introduced "Don," our junior enlisted person, to proceed with the presentation, and then I sat down. For about 30 minutes, "Don" maneuvered through all the slides and spoke in a clear, articulate voice. In the end, he had nailed the presentation. A few days later during the inspection, the senior IG official told me that he had never seen such a move by a unit commander. He was impressed that I had chosen the junior enlisted person to give the important first day orientation. I never told him that it might be even more significant considering "Don" circumstance only a few weeks earlier. In the end, we received an overall "Excellent" rating and scored "Outstanding" ratings on two of the individually evaluated areas.

I led in a way to what we are referring to as the Elvis Leadership Tip. I primarily used influence factors such as rewards, sharing knowledge, and forging personal relationships to build a good morale in the unit. I normally kept the other forms of power, my authority and ability to discipline, in abeyance. When warranted, I did use both as in this case to punish the young troop for his indiscretions. When done, I put those fingers (influence factors) away and got back to leading with a positive approach. I did not hold a grudge when people like "Don" made a mistake. In his case, he was still a valuable member of our unit and he deserved to be treated with respect and dignity.

Final Thoughts on Elvis-type Gesture as a Leadership Tip

I mentioned at the start of the book that if a concept is *simple*, we can remember it. If we can *remember* the concept, we can put into *practice*. The Talk to the Hand Leadership Concept uses a simple analogy of our own fingers on our hand to represent the various influence factors at a leader's disposal.

Similarly, I use the Elvis Leadership Tip as a means to remind us which influence factors we should use on a regular and proactive basis, and which ones are better used on a selective basis when warranted.

As a result, we are now in a good position to again look at

Brenda's signatures, but this time comparing all three of them. The first one reflects her signature when only two fingers are used (the "tough boss" approach) that represents only discipline and authority power factors.

The second signature below reflects Brenda's signature when only three fingers are used (the "likeable boss" approach) that indicates use of rewards, knowledge, and building a personal relationship. It is noticeably better than the first signature.

The third and final signature reflects Brenda's signature when all five fingers are used (the "complete and balanced boss" approach). It in essence reflects signature 1 *plus* signature 2.

Signature 1 (*only* middle and ring fingers)

Signature 2 (*only* thumb, index, and pinky)

Signature 3 (using *all* fingers)

"To mobilize people, executives must utilize all the means – including Machiavellian ones – suited to the situation."[100]

Harvard Business Review article, "The Wise Leader"

I believe the key to success for a leader is balance. The Elvis tip provides us that balance by reminding us that although a leader possesses a wide range of influence factors, using the appropriate one at the appropriate time is essential. It is not one set (positive/proactive) or the other (negative/reactive); it is using *both* in a balanced fashion.

Now that we have analyzed the Talk to the Hand Leadership Concept and the Elvis Leadership Tip for our professional endeavors, we can even use both concepts in our personal life roles such as parenting. Our next chapter addresses that personal element of our life.

Chapter Nine

Talk to the Hand to Be a Better Parent

"From a mental point of view, balance means keeping all things in perspective, maintaining self-control, and avoiding excessive highs and lows that occur because of luck or misfortune. Balance means not permitting the things over which you have no control to adversely affect the things over which you do have control, and it means retaining your poise during times of turmoil and triumph."[101]

Coach John Wooden

I will be the first to admit there was an *imbalance* between my professional endeavors and my personal life. I tried a lot harder and focused 100 percent on the former, and did a lot less so with the latter. Winning an award like "Male Boss of the Year" through the Federal Woman's Program is a notable achievement, but I never deserved anything similar on the homefront.

Only over the last few years have I realized that, I should

have practiced the same principles I did with people at home, as I had with people at work. I do believe that the Talk to the Hand Leadership Concept can help provide the necessary balance in our various roles such as a parent. Even our Elvis Gesture Leadership Tip applies as much at home as the work place as we shall see later in this chapter.

The first issue we need to resolve is that people are people, regardless if they are at the work location or in your own home. Does your son or daughter have any less feelings or emotions than the people you are trying to mentor at work to succeed in their career? Yet, for some reason we sometimes tend to want to get "off the clock" as a leader when we walk through the front door of our homes. Let our spouse deal with the tough issues, "I'm beat," the reasoning goes. The people who are closet to us, often sharing the same blood, deserve the very best from us just as your people at work. I found this out way too late in life, but fortunately we can learn from our mistakes and move on. So with that said, let's continue Talking to the Hand.

Parenting: Leading Your Children

"The good news is that you are in a position of tremendous power in regard to influencing the development of your child. The bad news is that you are in a position of tremendous power in regard to influencing the development of your child."[102]

Dr. Phil McGraw

When my son Jason was born, I was all of nineteen years old. There were advantges to this arrangement to be sure. I am not certain who was more excited to play a game of catch or go to the video arcade, me or Jason. In hindsight though, I let some disadvantages creep into our relationship too. Later in life, I would "pal" around with him doing things that he was better off doing with his friends, not me. When a parent wants to be a "best friend" with their child, they are not as likely to put on their *parent hat* to exert their parenting authority or even administer necessary discipline. Perhaps they could, but it makes it very difficult.

Even in the work environment, I cannot be a "best friend" to a subordinate because that can lead to fraternization – a military term that implies a breach of good order and discipline because of favoritism. If I were *too close* to someone, the logic goes, how could I then single the person out for necessary correction or discipline? If there is even a perception that is the case, then morale and team cohesion is going to suffer. In the same manner, does your child need you as a best friend? He or she can have lots of friends, but your child only has one Father and one Mother.

On the other end of the spectrum, there is little evidence that supports the belief that being a mean or tough boss is associated with any kind of business success in the workplace. Why wouldn't the same hold true for being a mean or tough parent in the homefront? Again in our Talk to the Hand model, we are not saying to *never* use authority and discipline (being the tough parent). When it comes to supervising the workforce or in the homefront supervising children, seeking balance is crucial. Dr. James Dobson, in his book *The New Dare to Discipline*, says this:

"We come now to the foundational understanding on which the entire parent-child relationship rests. It is to be found in a careful balance between love and discipline. The interaction of those two variables is critical and is as close as we can get to a formula for successful parenting."[103]

Parenting: Use of Rewards

In chapter four, we encouraged leaders to serve their people "cake" or a "break," by offering a tangible reward for their followers' tangible results. *Cake* symbolized a short-term treat such as money, time-off, or even a simple thank you. Praise, in particular is important, because as parents we tend to concentrate on a child's shortcomings and not enough on the times that they are succeeding.

As Dr. Phil noted in his book, *Family First*:

"Far too often, kids hear about what they've done wrong. Constant faultfinding can and will shoot down a child's sense of self-worth and initiative. If you're criticizing, you're not praising. You must start praising your children for positive behavior."[104]

Our employees appreciate kind words and thanks, but they also value other tangible rewards. In the same manner, so do our children. In Dr. Charles Stanley's *Handbook for Christian Living*, he offers the following advice:

"...work out a system of rewards for your children as well. Just as we avoid behavior that is punished, we repeat behavior that is rewarded. Extending a teenager's curfew in response to the faithfulness to come home on time is an appropriate reward. As adults, we look forward to bonuses at work, and there is nothing wrong with that. There is no reason that our children can't look forward to bonuses, either."[105]

To the workforce, a *break* means looking for an opportunity to foster professional development. As a parent, we can also seek ways for our children to grow in their personal development. In his book, *Father and Child Reunion*, Dr. Warren Farrell emphasizes the role that a father plays in a child's growth:

"Onr of the most powerful contributions many fathers make to their families is getting the children involved in team sports. Not sports, but team sports...teach(es) children a balance between cooperation and competition, between 'letting go' and 'rules of the game,' between fun and discipline, between winning and being a good loser, and between inspiration and perspiration...".[106]

Some children prefer not to participate in extracurricular activities. Parents need to be persistent in facilitating *break* opportunities such as dance, piano lessons, and Bible School.

Parenting: Sharing Knowledge (especially important)

In my professional career, there were times when I would walk into my supervisor's office and unload a problem or dilemma that I was facing at the time. There were two types of bosses. Those that tried to *solve* the problem for me and literally pick up the phone and start taking action. Or those that would *listen* more than speak and let me work out my own problems. The ideal boss is the latter and not the former. One of my favorite quotes is: "Give a man a fish, and you feed him for a day. Teach him how to fish, and you feed him for a lifetime." I believe the same holds true for parents and teaching their children wisely.

In their book, *The Pearls of Love and Logic for Parents and Teachers*, Jim Fay and Foster Cline offer valuable insight in how we instruct our children.

"Children have too few opportunities to learn about and practice for the real world. These opportunities present themselves most often as problems to solve or decisions to make. Each time I move into the situation, solve the problem, or rescue the child, *I have stolen one of the child's growth experiences*. He or she is now less prepared to face the real world than if I had been there with understanding and the question, 'What are you going to do about it'?"[107]

Fay and Cline continue with five basic steps to share your own knowledge in a constructive manner that teaches your children "how to fish."[108]

1. Show understanding.
2. Ask, "How are you going to solve the problem?"
3. Share some choices.
4. Help him/her look at the consequences.
5. Give the child permission to solve it or not solve it.

Allowing our children the *opportunity to fail* is the sign of a parent with courage, patience, and most important of all, love. Ultimately, it is the best type of knowledge that we can pass on to our children, better than even *solving* their specific problem at the time.

Parenting: Use of Discipline and Punishment

Here is where the Beyond a Reasonable Doubt or BARD rule comes in handy for a parent. You can use the BARD discipline rule as a simple, yet powerful guide in determining when to discipline. We adapted it to fit your role as a parent.

> ~~~~~~~~~~~
> The BARD Discipline Rule
> Never discipline your children unless
> you are *beyond a reasonable doubt* they
> deserve it.

The BARD discipline rule keeps your credibility high in several ways. First, we are better off by not overreacting too quickly. We are at our worst, both as workplace leaders and home front parents, when we make decisions based on raging emotions. The BARD rule slows you down enough to gather the facts and determine if your child is at fault *beyond a reasonable doubt*.

Secondly, by following the Beyond a Reasonable Doubt or BARD rule, when we determine the facts are there, we *must* discipline accordingly (and not with cruel and unusual punishment). When we are upset or angry, we are likely to administer *cruel and unusual punishment*, such as shouting "You are grounded for a year!" In most cases, after cooling off after a time, we realize we may have overreacted with our discipline. Our choices are to back down with our original punishment (not a great option) or to go ahead and enforce it anyway (probably a worse option). The key is to be consistent.

In her book, *Don't Be Afraid to Discipline*, Dr. Ruth Peters encourages parents to be consistent in their disciplinary approach. She notes the following:

"I've found that the least effective parenting style is the parent who is *consistently inconsistent* – changing tactics, demands, and consequences to meet his or her own immediate needs and moods."[109]

Parenting: Using and Keeping Authority

In the same manner that leaders draw lines in the sand to discourage inappropriate behavior in the workplace (sexual harassment, racial discrimination), parents must use their parental authority to draw boundary lines for their children.

Use Parental Authority to *draw* the line:

David Jeremiah, a senior pastor and best-selling author, noted the following when it comes to parents and authority.

"If you talked to as many young people as I do, you would soon discover that most who grow up in homes without boundaries or restrictions would give anything for some tangible evidence that Mom and Dad care enough to insist on knowing where their kids are and what they are doing. Boundaries are critical if we're to communicate love to our children."[110]

A parent must always keep their authority as Mom and Dad and never give it away unnecessarily. I believe if you try and be "best friends" with your children, that is exactly what you are doing. You are *overusing the pinky* (relationship) and *minimizing the ring finger* (authority). You certainly should spend quality time with your children and encourage them continously. However, if you pursue the "best friend" route, that is how your child might begin to see you. Only a parent can draw boundary lines, not a best friend.

Parenting: Forging a Relationship with our Children

As we encouraged a manager to have fun at work to build up our relationship (pinky power), we can do the same at home. In his book, *Active Parenting*, Michael Popkin relays the following advice:

"Having fun is a common way for relationships to begin and to grow. When you share a happy experience with your child, each of you subcosciously associates that pleasurable feeling with the other, and your relationship is strengthened."[111]

Popkin, a Director of the Active Parenting Program, goes on to share that having fun tends to get pushed aside by other demands. He continues, "Unfortunately, as parents become busier and busier, they often find less and less time for having fun with their children. They use their limited time to take care of what they view as more essential tasks of being a parent: cleaning, cooking, shopping, and discipline."[112]

What obviously is missing in this situation is a balanced approach, an approach that the Talk to the Hand Leadership Concept promotes at both work and at the homefront.

Parenting: Using the Elvis Gesture

Two-time heavyweight boxing champion George Foreman once noted that, "Parents need to correct their children but they also need to make an equal amount of time to encourage them."[113] In other words, there should be a balance, an equilabrium among the influence factors that a parent posseses.

In our Elvis Gesture Leadership Tip, we are *proactive* in three influence factors involving rewards, sharing knowledge, and forging a relationship. We are *reactive* (pulling the two middle fingers in) for using discipline and exerting authority. Once again, we can apply the Elvis Gesture Leadership Tip as a guide to our leadership role, or in this case in the role of parenting. We replaced the word leader with the word parent.

Be an upbeat _parent_ until the time calls for you to be otherwise.

Applying the Elvis Gesture Tip as a parent means being an upbeat person until necessary to do otherwise – same as at work.

The Parenting Handbook (The Bible)

I believe that the Bible is applicable, and in fact most valuable, to our daily life. It is especially important in guiding our role as a parent. Turning to the various Bible teachings on effective parenting that come from Deuteronomy, Ephesians, 2 Timothy, Proverbs, and others, we can develop a form of mission statement for both the Mom and Dad to use as a guide in how we lead our children.

Mission Statement for a Mom

~~~~~~~~~~

As a Mom, I am to always be available for my children and to be involved with their lives, to teach them God's words and to train them to discover the strengths He has given them, to discipline them firmly but fairly, to nurture them with unconditional love but enough freedom to fail on occasion, and to finally, to always model with integrity in my own life.

Mission Statement for a Dad

> ~~~~~~~~~~~~
>
> As a Dad, I must always put the Lord God first in my life, and to show my children to fear the Lord so that they may follow His decrees and commandments, to use the Bible to teach righteousness, to train my child when he is young so he will not turn from it when old, not to provoke my child harshly, but to educate and constructively discipline them.

Notice how the parent mission statements provides balance across the full use of the influence factors shown below. As parents, since we are to pass on our wisdom to our children who are still developing, the one influence factor that is used more often is sharing knowledge.

Rewards (reward of time, reward of opportunity)
- Always be available for my children and to be involved with their lives
- Enough freedom to fail on occasion

Sharing Knowledge (acquire, share, and be trusted)

- To teach them God's words
- Train them to discover the strengths He has given them
- Show my children to fear the Lord so that they may follow His decrees and commandments
- Use the Bible to teach righteousness
- Train my child when he is young so he will not turn from it when old

Using Punishment (Benefit of Doubt, Beyond Reasonable Doubt)

- Discipline them firmly but fairly
- Educate and constructively discipline them

Status and Authority (use for others, draw a line in the sand)

- Put the Lord God first in my life
- Not to provoke my child harshly

Forging Relationships (communicate, EQ tactics)

- Nurture them with unconditional love
- Always model with integrity in my own life

Final Thoughts on Leading your Children

"Pull the string, and it will follow wherever you wish. Push it, and it will go nowhere at all."[114]

Dwight D. Eisenhower

Being an upbeat boss who responds through authority or discipline only when they have to makes sense from a business perspective. People are more likely to follow if they know that you have their best interests at heart. As Colin Powell once said: "Take care of the people, and the people will take care of you." I believe that being positive to your children is also essential in the same manner as it is in the workplace.

In their book, *What Happy Working Mothers Know*, Greenberg and Avigdor, expand on the correlation between leading people at work and parenting. They offer the following advice to working Moms:

"You are the same person at home as at work. Your style of leadership, whether as CEO of your family or in the workplace, is basically the same. You will be most effective if you work with your authentic style."[115]

I too believe that authenticity is an important issue as a leader and a parent. Too many times, I see someone promoted to a supervisory position and feel they must change their normal style and become a "bad cop" or "tough boss." I do not think that works in the workplace *or* the home.

At the same time, a parent needs to love their children enough to discipline them to establish and enforce boundaries for them. Failing to act, or react as the case may be, is also a failure of leadership, as a parent or a manager.

The Talk to the Hand Leadership Concept reminds us that a leader has many forms of power available to use. As a parent, we have the same type of influence factors – rewards, knowledge, discipline, authority, and relational. The key for both a boss and a parent is a natural balance among the five and with the proper timing.

Chapter Ten

Conclusion

"Are you talking about Picasso? That's what I call him. When a guy can throw the ball where he wants to, anywhere, on any pitch, at any time in the count, that's painting. And no one paints like Maddux."[116]

Arizona outfielder Luis Gonzalez on pitcher Greg Maddux

Think for a moment, after reviewing the following list of notable persons and their professions. What do they have in common?

- Wilbur and Orville Wright (Inventors)
- Pablo Picasso (Painter)
- Paula Deen (Chef)
- Eric Clapton (Musician)
- Danica Patrick (Race car driver)
- Sanjay Gupta (Surgeon – commentator)
- Irving Berlin (Composer)
- Jennie Finch (Softball pitcher)

They all used their hands.

There is an *artisanship* that occurs in each of their chosen occupation, and that includes mastering the tools of their trade. A certain pitch, a precision cut, striking a piano key, the touch on a wheel, or a proper stroke of a brush can make the difference. The fingers are intricately linked to the person's mental capacity (brain), and then back again for proper execution. In essence, these persons talk to the hand: "Do this now, do it that way."

In baseball, the pitcher is an important player for the team, because his or her performance has a direct impact on whether the squad wins the game or not. As Orioles Manager Earl Weaver put it: "Nobody likes to hear it, because it's dull. But the reason you win or lose is darn near always the same – pitching."[117] To be *most* effective, a pitcher needs a full repertoire of pitches.

Using various fingers effectively increases that repertoire and the likelihood of winning. For example, a pitcher uses primarily the index and middle fingers (along with the thumb) to throw a fastball pitch. For a change-up pitch (an off-speed throw), the pitcher adds the pinky to the middle and index finger on top, and the thumb and pinky underneath. A palm ball uses four fingers held across the ball, and so on and so forth.

Imagine for a moment, if a baseball pitcher could deliver only *one* type of pitch. No matter how good that single pitch was (fastball, curveball, etc); he or she would not be as effective as a hurler who had a *full* repertoire of pitches. Part of the problem is that the pitcher would become so predictable that the batters would be able to tee off with their bats because every pitch is the same.

A good pitcher not only uses *various* pitches, but also determines which one is *best for the situation*. If the bases are loaded with no outs, a pitcher is seeking to get the batter to hit the ball on the ground to cause a double play or a force out at home plate. Therefore, a slider (ball going down) may be the optimal pitch to use. A pitcher with a full repertoire of available pitches is more likely to succeed at that moment than one who has only one or two available options (pitches). Pete Rose once made the following observation about several great pitchers:

"Hardest thrower – (Sandy) Koufax. Toughest competitor – Bob Gibson. Most complete pitcher – Juan Marichal. In a jam, Marichal could throw any one of five pitches for a strike."[118]

Similarly, a *complete leader* uses the full repertoire of available *power* (also five in this case) and is more likely to succeed.

> ~~~~~~~~~~~
> As in the case of the artisans cited, the softball pitcher, the chef, the painter, and the surgeon, it may take a lifetime to master the trade – and the tools that go with them. The same is true for a leader to master his or her tools.

A business leader, conversely, must still perform as an artisan, (leadership is an art, not a science) but without any use of their hands. That is the whole point. The Talk to the Hand Leadership Concept is a simple tool for leaders to use to assist them in their demanding role of influencing other people.

Throughout this book, we emphasized the importance of good balance and timing for a leader. In the Talk to the Hand Leadership Concept, the leader can use a variety of power and influence factors (represented by the five fingers) that include the following *tools of the leadership trade*:

- Using Rewards to motivate others (thumb)

- Sharing your Knowledge (index finger)

- Punish or Discipline when necessary (middle finger)

- Establishing and using Authority (ring finger)

- Forging a Relationship with others (pinky)

A leader does not obviously rely on the use of hands in the same manner as a baseball pitcher, or a composer, a carpenter, a musician, or even a surgeon. In their case, the brain and the fingers on their hands, work in harmony as one impacts the other.

- For a pitcher, to deliver a third strike on the baseball field.

- For a chef, to create a culinary masterpiece in the kitchen.

- For a surgeon, to save a life in the operating room.

As in the case of the artisans cited, it may take a lifetime to master the trade – and the tools that go with them. The same is true for a leader to master his or her tools. President John F. Kennedy once observed, "Learning and leading are indispensable to each other."

A leader may be good in one area (forging relationship with people) but lacking in another (administering discipline). That is okay, many people face the same challenge. Others may be fine with using authority, but somehow cannot offer a simple thank you as a reward for good performance. If that is your case, you are not alone, trust me.

The key is to keep working at developing *your* leadership repertoire of power and influence factors, and that you *choose* to use them. As always, seeking a good balance among the power factors is just as important. Each leader is unique and should use these influence factors in a manner that is a best fit for them. Be yourself.

We close the book with a final look at the signature test that I gave Brenda and showed in earlier chapters. The top one is *unrepresentative* of Brenda's true signature since she did not use all five fingers. The second one below it represents her true signature. It does so because she used *all of her fingers naturally* and it captures her utmost potential.

Signature 1 (only two fingers):

Brenda J Garcia (handwritten signature)

Signature 2 (using all fingers):

Brenda J Garcia (handwritten signature)

I encourage you to work on your own *leadership signature*, and my hope is that it always reflects your *fullest repertoire* of power and influence as a leader. Doing so will benefit you, the people you serve with, and help contribute to your organization's success.

Good luck in all your leadership endeavors.

Endnotes

Introduction
1. Found at website, Brainy Quote,
   http://www.brainyquote.com/quotes/
2. John Wooden and Steve Jamison, *The Essential Wooden: A Lifetime of Lessons on Leaders and Leadership* (New York: McGraw-Hill, 2007), 5.

Chapter 1 (Gift of Fingers and Hands)
3. Found at website, Brainy Quote,
   http://www.brainyquote.com/quotes/
4. Jenna Johnson, "Hearts, hands find no need for speech," *The Washington Post*, December 13, 2010, p B1.
5. Doris Kearns Goodwin, *Team of Rivals: The Political Genius of Abraham Lincoln* (New York: Simon and Schuster, 2005), 499.
6. Ibid.
7. Ibid.
8. Jack Canfield, Mark Hansen, and Sidney Slagter, *Chicken Soup for the Veteran's Soul: Stories to Stir the Pride and Honor the Courage of Our Veterans* (Deerfield Beach: Health Communications, Inc., 2001), 6-7.
9. Ibid.
10. Ibid.
11. Ibid.
12. Found at website, Brainy Quote,
    http://www.brainyquote.com/quotes/
13. Found at website, Sports ESPN,
    http://sports.espn.go.com/nfl/news/
14. Dan Hellie, "Matt Bradley on the Real Pains of Rehab," *NBC Washington*, Jan 24, 2011

15. Found at website, Great Quotes.com,
    http://www.great-quotes.com/quote/879783

Chapter 2 (Talk to the Hand Leadership Concept)

16. Found at website, Brainy Quote,
    http://www.brainyquote.com/quotes/
17. Jeffrey Pfeffer and John Veiga, "Putting people first for organizational success," *The Academy of Management Executive*, May 1999
18. John Wooden and Steve Jamison, *The Essential Wooden: A Lifetime of Lessons on Leaders and Leadership* (New York: McGraw-Hill, 2007), 8-9.
19. Ibid.
20. Ibid.
21. Bil Holton, *Leadership Lessons of Robert E. Lee* (New York: Gramercy Books, 1995)
22. Joseph Garcia, *The Leader's Pyramid: a balanced and consistent approach to leadership* (Bloomington: AuthorHouse, 2010), 70-73.

Chapter 3 (Thumbs Up: Using Rewards)

23. Steve Chandler and Scott Richardson, *100 Ways to Motivate Others: How Great Leaders Can Produce Insane Results Without Driving People Crazy* (Franklin Lakes: Career Press), 207.
24. Alfie Kohn, *Punished by Rewards: The Trouble with Gold Stars, Incentive Plans, As, Praise, and Other Bribes* (New York: Houghton Mifflin Company, 1993), 27.
25. John P. Kotter, "What Leaders Really Do," *Harvard Business Review* (Leadership Insights Collection, 2010), 31.
26. Found at website, Brainy Quote,
    http://www.brainyquote.com/quotes/

27. Found at website, Quote Album,
    http://quotealbum.com/author/E.-M.-Cioran-Quotes

28. Pat Williams, *The Leadership Wisdom of Solomon: 28 Essential Strategies for Leading with Integrity* (Cincinnati: Standard Publishing, 2010), 83.

Chapter 4 (Index Finger: Sharing Knowledge)

29. Found at website, ThinkExist.com
    http://thinkexist.com/quotation/in_today-s_environment-hoarding_knowledge/150958.html

30. Stephen M.R. Covey and Rebecca Merrill, *The Speed of Trust: The One Thing That Changes Everything* (New York: Free Press, 2008), 93.

31. Found at website,
    http://www.rayfairman.com/index.php?option=com_content&task=view&id=36&Itemid=2

32. Stephen M.R. Covey and Rebecca Merrill, *The Speed of Trust: The One Thing That Changes Everything* (New York: Free Press, 2008), 105.

33. Found at website, ThinkExist.com
    http://thinkexist.com/quotation/

34. Found at website, Brainy Quote,
    http://www.brainyquote.com/quotes/

35. Glenn Beck, *Being George Washington: The Indispensable Man, as You've Never Seen Him* (Threshold Editions: New York, 2011), 148.

36. Ibid.

37. Ronald Heifetz and Marty Linsky, "A Survival Guide for Leaders," *Harvard Business Review* (Leadership Insights Collection, 2010), 74-75.

38. Tony Zinni and Tony Koltz, *Leading the Charge: Leadership Lessons from the Battlefield to the Boardroom* (New York:

Palgrave MacMillan, 2009).

39. Jim Shaffer, "Always Tell the Truth," *Communication World*, Apr 1995

40. Stephen R. Covey, *First Things First* (New York: Simon & Schuster, 1994), 240.

41. Tony Dungy and Nathan Whitaker, *The Mentor Leader: Secrets to Building People and Teams That Win Consistently* (Carol Stream: Tyndale House Publishers, 2010), 71.

42. Found at website, Air Force Academy http://www.usafa.af.mil/

43. *The Washington Post*, The Fed Page, May 30, 2011

44. Found at website, ThinkExist.com http://thinkexist.com/quotation/

45. Nancy Lieberman, *Playbook for Success: A Hall of Famer's Business Tactics for Teamwork and Leadership* (Hoboken: John Wiley and Sons Publishing, 2010), 109.

46. Marshall Goldsmith, *What Got You Here Won't Get You There* (New York: Hyperion, 2007), 90.

47. Pat Williams, *The Winning Combination: 21 Keys to Coaching and Leadership Greatness* (Monterey: Coaches Choice, 2010), 102.

48. William A. Cohen, *The Art of the Leader* (Englewood Cliffs: Prentice Hall, 1990), 65.

Chapter 5: (Middle Finger: Discipline)

49. Found at website, Brainy Quote, http://www.brainyquote.com/quotes/

50. John Maxwell, *Developing the Leaders Around You* (Nashville: Thomas Nelson Publishing, 2000), 125.

51. Amy C. Edmonson, "Strategies for Learning from Failure," *Harvard Business Review*, April 2011.

52. Ibid.

53. Doris Kearns Goodwin, *Team of Rivals: The Political Genius of Abraham Lincoln* (New York: Simon and Schuster, 2005), 529.
54. Ibid, 377-378.
55. Ibid, 485.
56. Nick Ragone, *Presidential Leadership: 15 Decisions That Changed the Nation* (Amherst: Prometheus Books, 2011), 175.
57. Ibid, 176.
58. Ibid, 180.
59. Ibid, 181.
60. Ibid, 179.
61. Nancy Lieberman, *Playbook for Success: A Hall of Famer's Business Tactics for Teamwork and Leadership* (Hoboken: John Wiley and Sons Publishing, 2010), 155.
62. Bil Holton, *Leadership Lessons of Robert E. Lee* (New York: Gramercy Books, 1995), 145.
63. Tony Dungy and Nathaniel Whitaker, *Quiet Strength: The Principles, Practices, and Priorities of a Winning Life* (Carol Stream: Tyndale House Publishers, 2007), 105.

Chapter 6 (Ring Finger: Status and Authority)
64. Found at website, University of Cornell Law School, http://topics.law.cornell.edu/wex/marriage
65. Ibid.
66. Oren Harari, *The Powell Principles: 24 Lessons from Colin Powell Battle-Proven Leader* (New York: McGraw-Hill, 2005), 39.
67. Pat Williams, *The Leadership Wisdom of Solomon: 28 Essential Strategies for Leading with Integrity* (Cincinnati: Standard Publishing, 2010), 22.
68. Ibid, 11-12.

69. Ibid.

70. Ibid, 18-19.

71. Lorin Woolfe, *The Bible on Leadership: From Moses to Matthew – Management Lessons for Contemporary Leaders* (New York: American Management Association, 2002), 180-181.

72. Ibid.

73. Bill Walsh, *The Score Takes Care of Itself: My Philosophy of Leadership* (New York: The Penguin Group, 2010), 119.

74. Pat Williams, *The Winning Combination: 21 Keys to Coaching and Leadership Greatness* (Monterey: Coaches Choice, 2010).

Chapter 7 (Pinky Finger: Forging a Relationship)

75. Tony Zinni and Tony Koltz, *Leading the Charge: Leadership Lessons from the Battlefield to the Boardroom* (New York: Palgrave MacMillan, 2009).

76. Oren Harari, *The Powell Principles: 24 Lessons from Colin Powell Battle-Proven Leader* (New York: McGraw-Hill, 2005), 3.

77. Nancy Lieberman, *Playbook for Success: A Hall of Famer's Business Tactics for Teamwork and Leadership* (Hoboken: John Wiley and Sons Publishing, 2010), 108.

78. Found at website, Brainy Quote, http://www.brainyquote.com/quotes/

79. Daniel Goleman, "What Makes a Leader?" *Harvard Business Review* (Leadership Insights Collection, 2010), 36.

80. Ibid.

81. Ibid, 44.

82. Ibid, 37.

83. Ibid, 44.

84. John Cleese, "And Now for Something Completely

Different," *Management Review*, May 1991, 50-53.

85. Steve Chandler, *100 Ways to Motivate Others: How Great Leaders can Produce Insane Results Without Driving People Crazy* (Franklin Lakes: Career Press, 2008), 156.

86. Oren Harari, *The Powell Principles: 24 Lessons from Colin Powell Battle-Proven Leader* (New York: McGraw-Hill, 2005), 89.

87. Michael Burchell and Jennifer Robin, *The Great Workplace: How to Build It, How to Keep It, and Why It Matters* (San Francisco: Jossey-Bass Publishing, 2011), 139-141.

88. Jim Kouzes and Barry Posner, *A Leader's Legacy* (San Francisco: Jossey-Bass Publishing, 2006), 57-59.

89. Ibid.

90. Mark Sanborn, *You Don't Need a Title to be a Leader: How Anyone, Anywhere, Can Make a Positive Difference* (Colorado Springs: Waterbrook Press, 2006), 58.

91. William Peace, "The Hard Work of Being a Soft Manager," *Harvard Business Review* (Leadership Insights Collection, 2010), 104.

92. Margaret Heffernan, *Women on Top: How Women Entrepreneurs are Rewriting the Rules of Business Success* (New York, Penguin Books, 2007), 113.

Chapter 8 (The Elvis Leadership Tip)

93. Michael Burchell and Jennifer Robin, *The Great Workplace: How to Build It, How to Keep It, and Why It Matters* (San Francisco: Jossey-Bass Publishing, 2011), 206-207.

94. Steve Chandler, *100 Ways to Motivate Others: How Great Leaders can Produce Insane Results Without Driving People Crazy* (Franklin Lakes: Career Press, 2008), 79.

95. Ibid.

96. Found at website, Brainy Quote,

http://www.brainyquote.com/quotes/

97. "The Science Behind the Smile," *Harvard Business Review*, January-February 2012, 85-90.

98. Jim Kouzes and Barry Posner, *A Leader's Legacy* (San Francisco: Jossey-Bass Publishing, 2006), 58-59.

99. Ibid, 60.

100. Ikujiro Nonaka and Hirotaka Takeuchi, "The Wise Leader: How CEOs can learn practical wisdom to help them do what's right for their companies – and society," *Harvard Business Review*, May 2011, 58-67.

Chapter 9 (Talk to the Hand to be a Better Parent)

101. John Wooden and Steve Jamison, *The Essential Wooden: A Lifetime of Lessons on Leaders and Leadership* (New York: McGraw-Hill, 2007), 121.

102. Phil McGraw, *Family First: Your Step-by-Step Plan for Creating a Phenomenal Family* (New York: Free Press, 2005), 257.

103. James Dobson, *The New Dare to Discipline* (Wheaton: Tyndale Publishing, 1992), 48.

104. Phil McGraw, *Family First, Your Step-by-Step Plan for Creating a Phenomenal Family* (New York: Free Press, 2005), 37.

105. Charles Stanley, *Handbook for Christian Living* (Nashville: Thomas Nelson, Inc.,1996), 393.

106. Warren Farrell, *Father and Child Reunion: How to Bring the Dads we Need to the Children we Love* (New York: Jeremy Tarcher/Putnam, 2001), 58..

107. Jim Fay and Foster Cline, *The Pearls of Love and Logic for Parents and Teachers* (Golden: The Love and Logic Press, 2000), 2-3.

108. Ibid.

109.Ruth Peters, *Don't Be Afraid to Discipline* (New York: St. Martin's Press, 1997), 17.

110.David Jeremiah, *Hopeful Parenting: Encouragement for Raising Kids Who Love God* (Colorado Springs: David Cook, 2008, 46-47.

111.Michael Popkin, *Active Parenting* (New York: Harper Collins Publishing, 1987), 86.

112.Ibid.

113.George Foreman *God in my Corner* (Nashville: Thomas Nelson, 2007), 122-123.

114.Found at website, Brainy Quote, http://www.brainyquote.com/quotes/

115.Cathy Greenberg and Barrett Avigdor, *What Happy Working Mothers Know* (Hoboken: John Wiley & Sons, 2009), 177.

Chapter 10 (Conclusion: Tools of the Trade)

116.Wayne Stewart, The Gigantic Book of Baseball Quotations (New York: Skyhorse Publishing, 2007), 272

117. Ibid, 229.

118. Ibid, 231.

Acknowledgements

To my beautiful and loving wife Brenda, for her continued inspiration, love, and encouragement. She is my trusted advisor in all matters, and her edits and feedback to this book were right on target and invaluable. It is as much her book as it is mine. To my dear friend L.C. Williams, mentioned numerous times throughout the book, for 25 years of friendship and support. His advice is also much appreciated. To my former co-worker and good friend Emery Hamilton, who not only reviewed the book and provided excellent edits and suggestions, he was part of numerous tips such as "the sandman" and "lightning bolt" references. Most importantly, I acknowledge our Lord's many blessings in my life, including the gift of salvation that comes only through His Son Jesus Christ.

Joseph Garcia was the first and only Chief Financial Officer (CFO) for FEMA Hurricane Katrina Gulf Coast Recovery operations in their New Orleans, Louisiana oversight office. He performed in this Senior Executive Service position for three years. His mantra was, "to not sacrifice the recovery mission, but to honor the sacrifices of the American taxpayers who entrusted us with their resources." He led the development of the first ever budget for recovery operations, and initiated a Good Stewardship Council for the entire Gulf Coast. At the time of his departure, the overhead cost ratio was down to six percent, significantly lower than the Office of Management and Budget expectation of 14 percent for disaster overhead costs, saving taxpayers millions of dollars.

He served previously as a CFO for a national nonprofit in Washington, DC, and is Board Chairman for a nonprofit that supports women and children who suffer from human rights abuses. Joseph spent 28 years in the Air Force where he served as a squadron commander, spent a tour at the Pentagon, was deployed for six months in the Middle East, and served in numerous overseas assignments including South Korea and Germany. While assigned to the Air Force Academy, he taught a Leadership course to upper-division cadets, in addition to being a Training Director and a Regional Director of Admissions. He retired at the rank of Lieutenant Colonel. He holds an Executive Masters in Leadership from Georgetown University, in Washington, D.C. His awards include the Federal Woman's Program Male Boss of the Year, Department of Defense Comptroller of the Year, and a Superior Mission Achievement award from the Department of Homeland Security. He and his wife, Brenda, reside near Washington, DC.

www.ingramcontent.com/pod-product-compliance
Lightning Source LLC
Chambersburg PA
CBHW060021210326
41520CB00009B/957